100% COTTON

T-SHIRT GRAPHICS

WRITTEN BY HELEN WALTERS
DESIGN BY TIM FLETCHER

 LAURENCE KING

CREATIVE

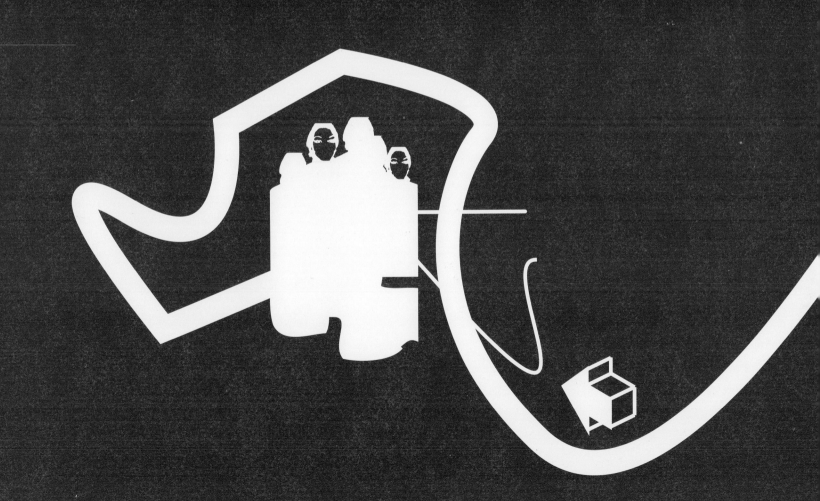

100% CONTENTS

ore than a cheap article of clothing, the T-shirt is a portable ad, its wearers declaring their political, musical or social affiliations for all the world to see. As a walking billboard or a medium for innovative graphics, provocative T-shirts invariably inspire a reaction; shocking, controversial or humorous graphics offend or amuse depending on your age, sex, political bent or mood that day. What started off as a humble piece of underwear has, thanks in part to the efforts of teen idols such as Marlon Brando and James Dean, become the standard wear of the young. And graphics, slogans and type have all had their part to play in maintaining its iconic status.

The first record of the T-shirt's existence comes from 1899, when a plain white cotton shirt formed an official part of the US navy uniform. By the 1930s, T-shirts, again plain white cotton, were becoming standard sporting wear at some American universities, while in 1939 printed T-shirts were used as part of the promotion for the film **The Wizard of Oz**, though apparently these were not wildly popular at the time. It wasn't really until after the Second World War that the practice of putting graphics onto shirts became widespread. During the war, GIs posted to the Pacific had worn T-shirts, known then as "T-types", as outerwear in an attempt to cope with the extreme heat. Most were plain white, but some were printed with the names of individual camps or divisions. The idea of wearing T-shirts as a kind of uniform was well and truly born.

Former GI-turned-designer and Hot Rodder, Ed "Big Daddy" Roth brought this tradition of printing T-shirts back to America after the end of the war. Specializing in customizing cars and attending car shows, he introduced the graphic T-shirt to a whole new audience. "All car clubs had plaques that featured the name of the club and a piece of art (Buccaneers had a pirate, etc.). I was a natural because at the car shows I'd elaborate on the art piece, and the more I exaggerated the artwork, the better the younger guys liked it," he explains. Roth's shirts became so popular that, in the end, demand hugely outweighed supply. So he developed a silk-screen machine "that spit shirts out like bullets", allowing him to produce greater numbers of the same designs. Today a whole industry still uses variations of those early machines. Roth adds proudly: "In 1960 there were very few people that wore decorated shirts. Today there are very few people that wear plain shirts!"

IN 1965 BUDWEISER WAS ONE OF THE FIRST MAJOR BRANDS TO USE T-SHIRTS AS A MARKETING TOOL, AND COMPANIES HAVE BEEN BUSILY PRODUCING T-SHIRTS WITH LOGOS OR BRANDING ON THEM EVER SINCE

This practice of using graphics on T-shirts was soon seized upon by marketing professionals the world over, who were keen to exploit the medium's potential to advertise and promote their products. In 1965 Budweiser was one of the first major brands to use T-shirts as a marketing tool, and companies have been busily producing T-shirts with logos or branding on them ever since. In the early 1970s London-based company Mr Freedom bought a short-term licence from Walt Disney to place characters such as Mickey Mouse and Donald Duck on T-shirts. "Disney were taken aback as they'd never been asked to license stuff for T-shirts before," explains Mr Freedom co-founder Trevor Miles. "They gave us a licence for a year and we started printing T-shirts with Goofy on them. We were extremely successful," he adds. Judging by the continued popularity of such T-shirts even today, Disney, which reclaimed the licence after the year was up, was also extremely successful.

But T-shirts are not simply a means of indoctrinating an unwary public into the ways of a certain brand or product. Artists were quick to catch on to their potential as a means of getting their work out into the public domain. In the 1970s Robert Crumb's counter-culture classic cartoons such as **Stoned Again** and **Keep on Truckin'** neatly summed up the bored mood of the hippy generation, while even later, pop artist Keith

Haring opened the Pop Shop to sell his images on a range of clothing and accessories. In a **Rolling Stone** interview with David Sheff in 1989, he explained the deliberate reasoning behind his store: "My work was starting to become more expensive and more popular within the art market. Those prices meant that only people who could afford big art prices could have access to the work. The Pop Shop makes it accessible." Years after Haring's death in 1990, the shop is still going strong.

What is put onto a T-shirt more often than not captures the spirit of a whole period of time. In the early 1970s, iron-on transfers of idols such as the Beatles or the Rolling Stones (whose lips and tongue logo, designed by John Pasch, is something of a modern-day icon) were hugely popular, reflecting the success of the bands and their music. Designers within the music industry have traditionally produced stunning graphics for album covers, and in many cases these images have also been printed directly onto T-shirts, with tour dates and venue details printed on the back. Wearing a band T-shirt was, and still is, an easy way for a fan to signal his or her loyalties, not just at a gig, but also later in the street and in everyday life. Other fans immediately recognize a kindred spirit by the graphic symbols on the T-shirt, while the band can make some real money from their fan base: on their 1981 world tour, the Rolling Stones made nearly half of their total $50 million from the sale of merchandise.

Adrian Shaughnessy, creative director of London design company Intro, has designed both record sleeves and T-shirts for many rock bands. "I like the idea of T-shirts acting as a sort of secret code for initiates only," he says. "This is the opposite effect from the one the big brand owners hope to achieve. My teenage son wears T-shirts of obscure bands like Melt Banana and By Their Dead You Shall Know Them. It's his way of signalling his interests, communicating with other like-minded people. People who like these bands stop him in the street to talk about their shared obsession. It's the T-shirt as social catalyst."

Paul Frank, whose Californian company Paul Frank Industries sells a huge range of shirts, agrees with Shaughnessy. "Someone will stop you and ask why you're wearing something. I have a shirt I bought at a thrift store that says 'What side?' on it. When I wear it, people regularly say 'What side?' to me. You can meet people that way."

Sheffield-based graphics company The Designers Republic used to create all the T-shirts for 1980s band Pop Will Eat Itself, very often a different shirt for each gig. "The more you invest in an idea, the more you live the lifestyle, the more you need to invest," says the company's founder, Ian Anderson. "With Pop Will Eat Itself, we created a new improved, more focused expression of their target market's existing image, which consolidated the identity for people identifying with the attitude of the band. The success was dependent on the voluntary tribal nature of the participants." It seems that the music industry has been particularly adept at exploiting the potential of the T-shirt. "Depending which side of the consumerist fence you're on, it's either a case of the purist music business of the 1970s continuing to grow into a multitasking, multinational entertainment industry, with more and more avenues opening to fleece the punter in a context where the artist's music is merely a by-product of the overall consumer brand," Anderson explains. "The alternative, less cynical, view is that the growing availability of technology and increased access to markets for both producers and consumers allows the fan a greater choice of goods and therefore more opportunities to invest in their favourite band/brand."

There have been a few crucial moments in T-shirt design history. While they became increasingly acceptable as an everyday article of clothing throughout the 1960s and 1970s, it was punk rock that really sealed their position as the standard clothing of a disenfranchised youth. Punk combined the forces of fashion, music and politics to create an electric environment. Designers Vivienne Westwood and Malcolm McLaren, arguably the mother and father of the movement, chose the T-shirt as a uniform for their followers. "The T-shirt was the basis of everything, everything else spun out from there," says McLaren now. "The T-shirt was the foundation, the one thing that defined a look, if you were dealing with the street culture of the new generation. The T-shirt was the beginning of every shop we had on the King's Road [Let It Rock, Sex and Seditionaries were three of McLaren and Westwood's shops]. We always started with 'What's the T-shirt going to look like?' That was the defining moment. Wearing a T-shirt is the simplest, cheapest and easiest way to make a statement visually about your state of mind." Just as Marlon Brando, exuding cool in black leather and a plain white T, and the chain-smoking, T-shirt-wearing James Dean had both unwittingly played their part in making it essential wear for a cool, rebellious youth, punk sealed the T-shirt's status as acceptable clothing for the new rebels with a cause.

"WEARING A T-SHIRT IS THE SIMPLEST, CHEAPEST AND EASIEST WAY TO MAKE A STATEMENT VISUALLY ABOUT YOUR STATE OF MIND."
MALCOLM MCLAREN

"THE BEAUTY OF T-SHIRT DESIGN AND CONSUMPTION IS THE LOVE-AT-FIRST-SIGHT NATURE OF THE IDEA/BUYER RELATIONSHIP. THESE AFFAIRS ARE PREDOMINANTLY SHORT-LIVED. THERE'S ALWAYS SOMETHING NEWER ON THE MARKET." IAN ANDERSON, THE DESIGNERS REPUBLIC

Westwood and McLaren's T-shirts are still thought by many to epitomize the power of the garment. Their graphics were chosen carefully and deliberately to have as much effect as possible on a staid, traditional and, in their eyes, hypocritical establishment. Their determination to make their point culminated in them taking "untouchable" icons and subverting them: on one T-shirt they printed a swastika, a crucifix and the Queen's head underneath the word "destroy". McLaren calls this the "ultimate punk rock T-shirt" and claims that his intention was to demystify the three images. Whether or not that actually happened, it was certainly a success, selling ten times as many as any of their other, more sexually explicit shirts, and it undoubtedly helped a frustrated youth searching for a voice. "It gave an ideology to punk rock, it was what everyone could access," McLaren explains. "Not every kid wanted to walk around with a huge naked penis, a huge pair of tits or an image of the Cambridge Rapist on their shirt. But they caught the politics. The demystification of icons like the swastika made them feel like an outlaw. It personified their anger, it had a force to it."

Some of their T-shirts enraged the authorities so much that the shop was frequently raided and kept under surveillance by the Special Branch; their T-shirts were considered likely to cause a breach of the peace. But the inexorable rise of this new "youth culture", along with the radical politics and the new "do-it-yourself" mentality that followed had a huge effect on T-shirt graphics. In the mid-1980s, Katharine Hamnett used oversized T-shirts printed with huge type to draw attention to issues such as the use of nuclear weapons like the Pershing missile. At about the same time, pop band Frankie Goes to Hollywood adopted a careful combination of music and politics, printing T-shirts with legendary slogans "Frankie Say Relax!" or "Frankie Say War! Hide Yourself", again printed on white in huge black type. Many causes and issues still choose to promote themselves with a printed T-shirt as an immediate way of reacting to a situation. During the London mayoral elections in 2000, design company Hybrid doctored a photograph of Che Guevara (which has itself adorned thousands of T-shirts), replacing his face with that of Ken Livingstone, the city's modern-day revolutionary. During the build-up to the 1999 presidential elections in Zimbabwe, a supporter of the opposition was murdered simply for wearing an anti-Robert Mugabe slogan on his T-shirt.

"T-shirts are cheap to produce and cheap to buy in stores. It's a utilitarian piece of clothing," says cultural commentator Aaron Rose, director of the Alleged Gallery in New York. "They're so quick and easy to make; you can bang out a T-shirt immediately. It happens all the time. Princess Diana dies one minute, and there's a T-shirt for sale the next hour." Graffiti artist and designer Dave Kinsey of Black Market in San Diego was inspired to create T-shirt graphics after seeing the trial of Rodney King on television in 1992. On the front of the shirt, he printed an image of King's face with the words "King Victim". On the back was a photo of the officers beating him up with the caption "What the fuck is going on?" Printed up within a week, they were all sold within two days, with Kinsey regularly being stopped and asked about them. "They are like walking billboards. They describe one's personality and way of thinking and make a statement," he comments.

Of course, those statements don't always have to be right-on and politically correct. Indeed, for a youth still out to shock and offend, it's often better that they're not. Erik Brunetti has been designing T-shirts for his California-based clothing brand Fuct since the late 1980s, and along with many of the other skate/surf brands, his designs specialize in being provocative. "The one everyone really hates is 'litter creates jobs,'" Brunetti declares unrepentantly. "I always throw my wrappers away, and my friends always ask me why I do it. So I tell them if I didn't throw my litter out, then there would be no jobs for the working class. Trash men need jobs. And I do believe it to a certain extent. It's comedy, dark comedy. Another one everyone hates is one that says 'It's too late to recycle'. All the environmentalists get really upset about that."

Fuct is also a past master at lampooning and satirizing "big brand" culture. Its adaptation of the Ford logo to read "Fuct" is a classic example of this, while other good ones include "Doner Kebab" for Donna Karan or Hysteric Glamour's "Junkie's Baddy Powder" for Johnson's Baby Powder. It's another example of T-shirt graphics being used to get up the nose of a staid, uncomprehending establishment. Fashion label Red or Dead has regularly subverted existing brands (as well as made money out of selling ones adorned with its own logo). "I can't understand why anybody would want to wear a T-shirt that says 'Calvin Klein' or 'Armani' on it," says founder Wayne Hemingway. "You're paying a lot of money to someone who simply wants to make money, and you look like a tosser because you can't make up your mind what to wear." When controversial oil testing was taking place in the North Sea, Red or Dead tweaked the Shell logo to read "Hell" and sold the shirts in aid of Greenpeace. "They got really upset," Hemingway says, happily.

The crossover of surf and skate culture from niche market to everyday streetwear, together with the rise and rise of acid house music at the end of the 1980s, prompted another crucial moment in the T-shirt's design history. Designers began to use the T-shirt as a canvas for ideas that were not necessarily inspired by any politics or client, while people who would never have considered themselves fashion designers began to experiment with the medium. "People began making T-shirts in small batches for their friends, and it all became very entrepreneurial," says Fiona Cartledge, who ran the cult underground shop Sign of the Times, originally based in Kensington Market, London. "People were fed up and wanted to do something else. They had to get creative and meanwhile everyone had to get money to go to the raves and the clubs. They wanted to feel a part of the scene and if you created a T-shirt, you became a part of it. You sold them to your mates and suddenly half a club was in your design. It was a

ONE PROUD OWNER OF A T-SHIRT WITH SOME DELIGHTFUL JAPANESE WRITING ON IT WAS MOST PUT OUT TO DISCOVER THAT HE WAS IN FACT WEARING A SHIRT THAT READ "FUCKING STUPID AMERICAN TOURIST". IT'S A DOG-EAT-DOG WORLD OUT THERE IN T-SHIRT LAND

phenomenally powerful experience." There was a real burst of new, fresh designs at this time. "It was all happening so fast. Designs were been and done and dead in eight weeks," says Cartledge. Just as a T-shirt can be used to react to an event at lightning speed, so too can its appeal wear off very quickly. "The beauty of T-shirt design and consumption is the love-at-first-sight nature of the idea / buyer relationship. These affairs are predominantly short-lived, there's always something newer on the market," says Ian Anderson. "From the funkiest, geekiest graphic to the most profound philosophy, everything must pass. The future nostalgia action / reaction cycle is so complex now that everything in the history of T-shirt design appears to be happening right here, right now."

Since the early 1990s, the shape of the T-shirt has also evolved from the outsize, unisex, baggy clothing of the Hamnett or Frankie era. Instead, T-shirts have become skimpy, tight and sexy. As with all things fashion, however, some labels remain cooler and more popular than others. Aaron Rose keenly watches visitors to his gallery in New York and comments that it often resembles some kind of fashion show. "You'll see two people come in on two separate days wearing the exact same thing, but playing it off as if they're wearing something unique and different," he comments. "It's all showing off labels and that they're a part of this elite group. They're elite because they know the labels."

Meanwhile, a relatively new trend to have sprung up in Japan is the placing of English words onto T-shirts, regardless of whether or not these words actually mean anything. Fly Design has a whole range of these "nonsense" T-shirts, which apparently sell incredibly well in Asia. Westerners shouldn't feel too smug, however, as their complementary obsession with Japanese and Asian script is being exploited in turn. One proud owner of a T-shirt with some delightful Japanese writing on it was most put out to discover that he was in fact wearing a shirt that read "fucking stupid American tourist". It's a dog-eat-dog world out there in T-shirt land.

Better and more accessible printing facilities and the relatively cheap cost of plain T-shirts in the first place mean that more and more people are realizing that they can easily wear their own designs. Currently, there's something of a move back to the handmade aesthetic, with designers such as Einekoin in London specializing in creating one-off T-shirts with holes punched out of the material. Einekoin hold "roadshows" of work at which people can specify exactly how much and what customization of a garment they would like. It's a brave attempt to react against the increasingly homogeneous nature of our time, and one that reflects the T-shirt's continued status as a valid and effective forum for innovative design. Everyone has a favourite T-shirt, a baggy, threadbare, faded number that somehow always manages to avoid the charity shop bag. Because ultimately, whether you choose to wear a plain white T-shirt, a shirt with a Nike swoosh on it, or a death metal shirt, the T-shirt remains, quite literally, a cool item of clothing.

100%
SNAPS

"NEXT TO THE HAIRCUT, THE T-SHIRT MUST SURELY RATE AS THE MOST IMPORTANT FORM OF PERSONAL SELF-EXPRESSION FOR MANKIND (NOT INCLUDING DANCING OR TALKING). SURELY THE UNIFORM OF THE WORLD." SO COMMENTS DESIGNER PAUL MCNEIL, WHOSE WORK FOR MAMBO AND KIDDER IS FEATURED ELSEWHERE IN THIS BOOK. MCNEIL IS ABSOLUTELY RIGHT, T-SHIRTS ARE HUGELY COMMON, WORN BY YOUNG AND OLD, MEN AND WOMEN IN EVERY CITY, TOWN AND VILLAGE ON THIS PLANET. DISPOSABLE CAMERAS WERE USED TO DOCUMENT THIS REALITY AROUND THE WORLD AND THE FOLLOWING PAGES ARE MADE UP OF IMAGES FROM AS FAR AFIELD AS BANGKOK AND LOS ANGELES. SKIN COLOURS MAY BE DIFFERENT, SLOGANS MAY APPEAR IN DIFFERENT LANGUAGES, BUT IT'S REMARKABLE HOW SIMILAR WE ALL ARE. IT REALLY IS A SMALL WORLD.

PHOTOGRAPHS WERE TAKEN IN AND BY: LOS ANGELES, USA: CARINA FELDMAN. NEW YORK, USA: LEIGH ANN BOUTWELL. PORTLAND, USA: HELEN WALTERS. DURBAN, SOUTH AFRICA: GARTH WALKER. LONDON, ENGLAND: ALLISON WIGHTMAN. FLORENCE, ITALY: TIM FLETCHER. TOKYO, JAPAN: CHIHARU WATABE AND KOH CHIHARA. SAPPORO, JAPAN: SHIN SASAKI. SYDNEY, AUSTRALIA: PAUL MCNEIL. FRANKFURT, GERMANY: MARKUS WEISBECK. BANGKOK, THAILAND: MIMI GRACHANGNETARA.

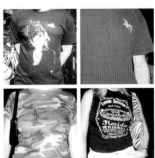

100% WORDS

fuct™

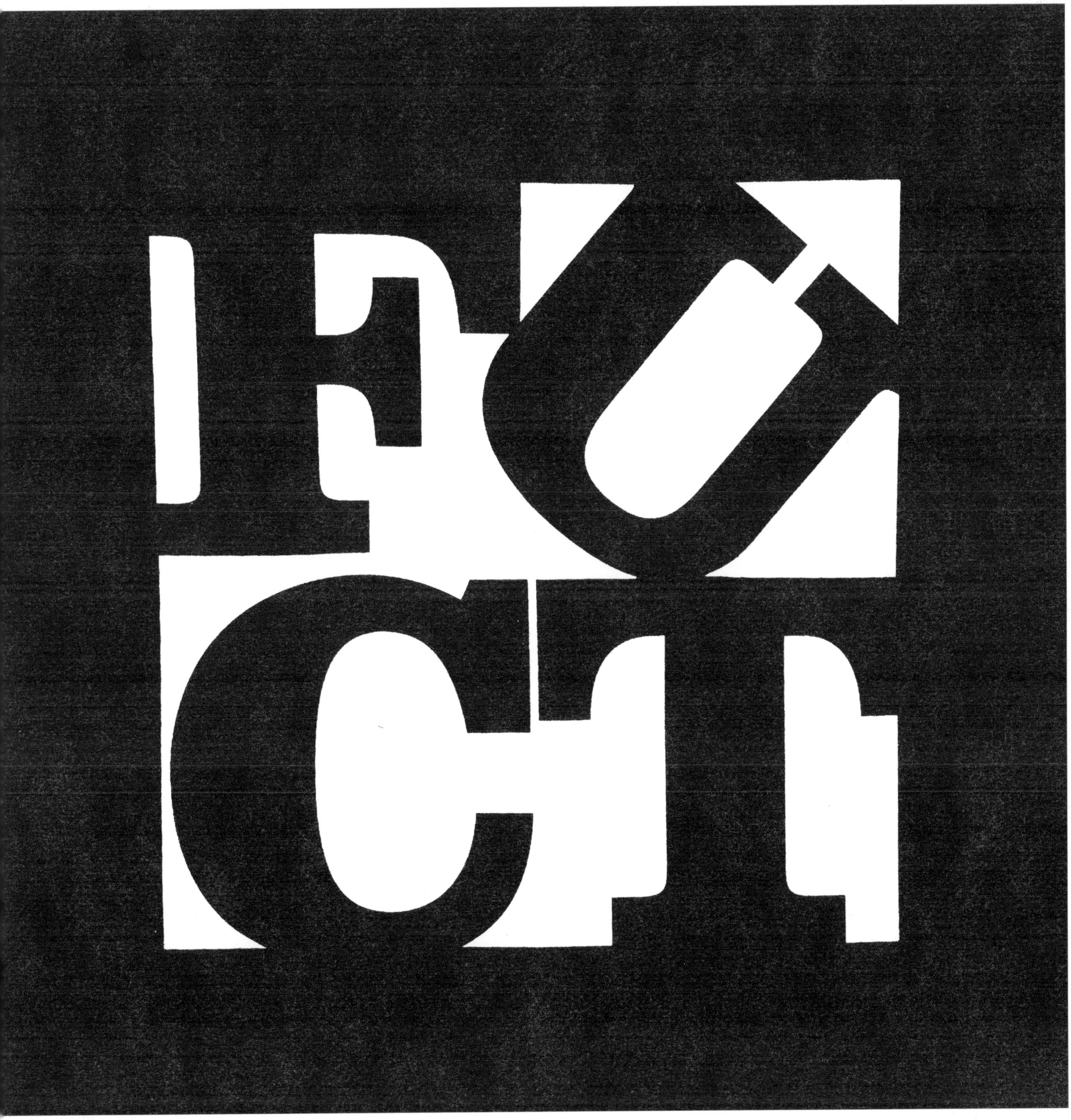
FU
CT

ERIK BRUNETTI HAS BEEN DESIGNING T-SHIRTS AND CLOTHING FOR HIS LABEL, FUCT, SINCE THE LATE 1980S. HIS T-SHIRTS OPENLY REFER AND PAY HOMAGE TO VISUAL
IMAGERY FROM BYGONE ERAS, OR "RIP THEM OFF", AS BRUNETTI PUTS IT. THE BRAND IS PARTICULARLY FAMOUS FOR ITS CASUAL APPROPRIATION AND ADAPTATION
OF EXISTING LOGOS OR ICONS, SUCH AS THE FORD MARQUE OR POP ARTIST ROBERT INDIANA'S "LOVE" (SHOWN PREVIOUS PAGE). PROVOCATIVE STATEMENTS ARE

DESIGNED TO SHOCK AND AMUSE, AND BRUNETTI ADMITS THAT WHEN HE WEARS ONE OF HIS OWN SHIRTS, HE OFTEN GETS STOPPED AND ASKED ABOUT THEM. "I USUALLY DON'T SPEAK TO THOSE PEOPLE BECAUSE MOST OF THEM ARE MORONS," HE SAYS MATTER-OF-FACTLY. "YOU CAN'T EXPLAIN SOMETHING TO AN IDIOT." ALL DESIGNS BY ERIK BRUNETTI. PREVIOUS SPREAD: THE ORIGINAL FUCT LOGO AND FUCT LOVE, 1999. THIS SPREAD: 01–03. 1999. 04. 1998. 05. 1995.

ONEPLAYER

01 02 03
03 04 DUTCH GRAPHIC DESIGN COMPANY DEPT CREATES SLOGAN-BASED T-SHIRTS THAT OPENLY REFER TO POP AND YOUTH CULTURE. BY TAKING ICONS AND SLOGANS INSTANTLY FAMILIAR TO THE COMPUTER-LITERATE YOUTH MARKET, THEY CREATE EYE-CATCHING CLOTHING FOR THOSE OF A CERTAIN MINDSET. "THE WAY SIMPLE WORDS PRINTED ON A T-SHIRT COMMUNICATE IS VERY POWERFUL TO US. WE SEE PEOPLE AS WALKING BILLBOARDS, ABLE TO SPEAK ABOUT WHERE THEY COME FROM OR WHAT THEY STAND FOR WITHOUT TALKING," EXPLAINS CO-FOUNDER MARK KLAVERSTIJN. ALL DESIGNS BY DEPT 01–03, 05: 1998. 04: 1996.

THE ROUTE
OF ALL OEUF
IS BEAUTIFUL

shoes come from box,
always in box.

OEUF SHIRTS TAKE THE IDEA OF WEARING A BRANDED T-SHIRT TO THE EXTREME: THERE ARE A MYRIAD OF DIFFERENT DESIGNS OF THE SAME BRAND NAME, WHICH ULTIMATELY MEANS NOTHING AT ALL (APART FROM "EGG" IN FRENCH, OF COURSE). T-SHIRTS WITH NONSENSE WRITING ON THEM ARE PARTICULARLY POPULAR IN JAPAN, WHERE PEOPLE SEEM TO SNAP UP ANYTHING ADORNED WITH NON-ASIAN WORDS. 01–05. DESIGNED BY ANDREW HARTWELL FOR OEUF: 01&04. 1999. 02&03. 1997. 05. 1998. 06. DESIGNED BY ANDREW HARTWELL, WILL BANKHEAD AND JAMES LAVELLE FOR L'OISEAU, 1997.

DESIGNERS FABIAN MONHEIM AND SOPHIA WOOD PICK RANDOM WORDS FROM A DICTIONARY TO CREATE T-SHIRTS FOR THE JAPANESE LABEL SPB. MEANWHILE, LONDON-BASED DESIGNER KAREN SAVAGE USES THE T-SHIRT AS A MEANS OF ANALYZING THE DIFFERENCES BETWEEN THE SEXES: SHE EMPLOYS VISUAL PUNS AND WITTY SLOGANS TO ENSURE STRONG, EYE-CATCHING T-SHIRTS. "I LIKE THE FACT THAT PEOPLE COMMUNICATE WITH EACH OTHER WHEN THEY'RE WEARING MY CLOTHES AND I'M NOT EVEN THERE," SAVAGE SAYS. "T-SHIRTS ARE LIKE FASHIONABLE SOUNDBITES." 01&02. DESIGNED BY FLEA, A SUBDIVISION OF FLY FOR SPB, 1998. 03–06. DESIGNED BY KAREN SAVAGE. 03&06. BIRD & COCK, 1997. 04. COUNCIL ESTATE PRINCESS, 2000. 05. BOLLOCKS, 1994.

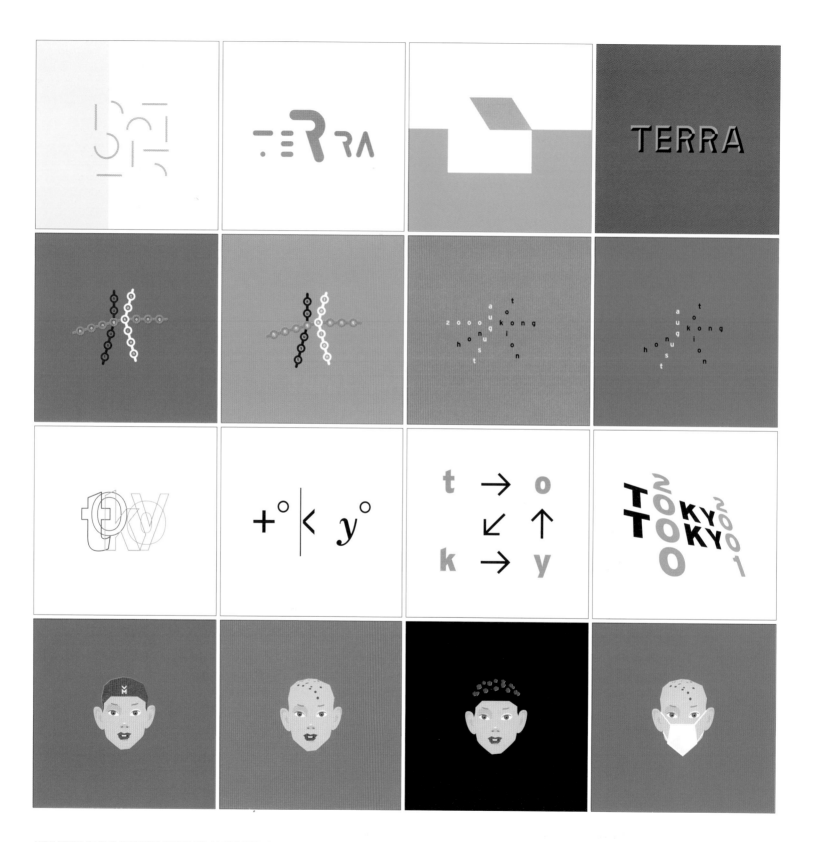

NEW YORK-BASED GRAPHIC DESIGNER ALEXANDER GELMAN USES TYPE THROUGHOUT HIS WORK, NOT LEAST FOR THE PROMOTIONAL T-SHIRTS HE CREATES FOR HIS OWN COMPANY, DESIGN MACHINE, AND FOR CLIENTS SUCH AS SONY AND THE INTERNET COMPANY TERRA. ALL DESIGNS BY ALEXANDER GELMAN AND KAORU SATO AT DESIGN MACHINE, 2000. ILLUSTRATIONS BY LUCY LYNN.

02 HOWIES CREATES WITTY, ORIGINAL T-SHIRTS AIMED AT AN AUDIENCE OF SKATE / BIKE KIDS. THEIR DONOR CARD T-SHIRT WAS LEGALLY BINDING WHEN YOU SIGNED IT
01 ON THE BACK. "IT'S WORN BY LONDON CYCLE COURIERS AND IF YOU SEE HOW THEY RIDE, YOU'LL UNDERSTAND WHY," SAYS COMPANY CO-FOUNDER, DAVID HIEATT.
THE "UNDERACHIEVER" SHIRT REFERS TO (AND MOCKS) THE ETHOS OF LARGE HAMBURGER CHAINS. CREATIVE DIRECTOR ON ALL DESIGNS WAS DAVID HIEATT. 01.
'UNDERACHIEVER DESIGNED BY SASSY. 02. DONOR CARD DESIGNED BY DAISY CRESSWELL, 1995–2000.

LONDON CLOTHING COMPANY SILAS COMMISSIONS DIFFERENT ILLUSTRATORS AND GRAPHIC DESIGNERS TO CREATE IMAGES ON A CERTAIN THEME: HORROR FOR SPRING / SUMMER 2000, WHILE FOR AUTUMN / WINTER 2000 THEY INVENTED THEIR VERY OWN TOWN, SILAS. EACH T-SHIRT REPRESENTS THE IDENTITY OF ONE OF THE TOWN'S SINISTER GANGS, SUCH AS THE SILAS PREACHERS OR THE SILAS DOMINO PLAYAZ: THE CRIMINAL UNDERBELLY THAT WOULD REMAIN TACTFULLY UNMENTIONED IN ANY TOURIST BROCHURE. IT'S A TACTIC THAT RUSSELL WATERMAN, CO-FOUNDER OF SILAS, BELIEVES TO BE MORE INTERESTING THAN SIMPLY

CHURNING OUT ANOTHER T-SHIRT BEARING A SILAS LOGO. "EVERYONE JUST WANTS A DIFFERENT VARIATION OF THE SILAS LOGO, BUT THIS IS A LOT MORE SOPHISTICATED," HE SAYS. "EACH OF THE GRAPHICS IS PICKED BECAUSE IT LOOKS STRONG ON ITS OWN AND IT FITS THE CONCEPT." 01–05. DESIGNED BY MARTIN WEDDERBURN, JAMES JARVIS, MARK FOSTER, BEN SANSBURY, WILL SWEENY AND FERGUS PURCELL, 2000.

01	02	03
04	05	

FOUNDED IN JAPAN BY NOBU KITAMURA IN 1984, THE CLOTHING LABEL HYSTERIC GLAMOUR USES GRAPHICS INSPIRED BY THE POP, PSYCHEDELIC AND ROCK ERAS, BUT HAPPILY PLUNDERS AND SUBVERTS COMMERCIAL GRAPHICS TOO ("JUNKIE'S BADDY POWDER" FOR "JOHNSON'S BABY POWDER"). 01–03. DESIGNED BY NOBU KITAMURA. 01&02. 1994. 03. 1992. 04. DESIGNED BY STEPHAN WOLF, 2000. 05. DESIGNED BY FERGUS PURCELL, 1999.

metal

TRANS FORMER

IM EVIL

PANDA MANIA
HYSTERIC

IN THE LATE 1980S, SHAWN STUSSY WAS A SURFER WHO USED TO SHAPE BOARDS FOR FRIENDS AND LOCALS IN LAGUNA BEACH, CALIFORNIA. HIS LOGO WAS MADE UP OF A GRAFFITI-STYLE TAG OF HIS OWN SURNAME, AND BEFORE TOO LONG HE BEGAN TO PRINT THIS IMAGE ONTO T-SHIRTS. THE REST, AS THEY SAY, IS HISTORY, AND STÜSSY IS NOW A MASSIVELY SUCCESSFUL AND WELL-RESPECTED WORLDWIDE CLOTHING BRAND. ALL DESIGNS BY SHAWN STUSSY. 01&03, 2000. 02. 1988.

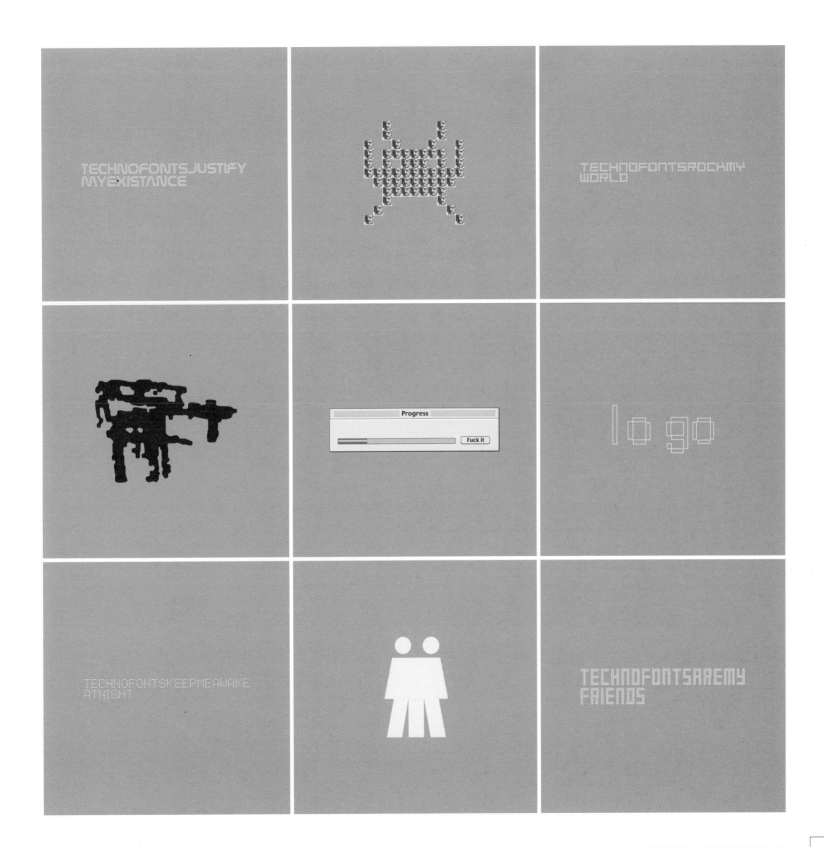

GRAPHIC DESIGN COMPANIES HAVEN'T BEEN SLOW TO PICK UP ON THE T-SHIRT'S POTENTIAL AS A VEHICLE FOR COMMUNICATION. LONDON DESIGN COMPANIES INSECT AND THINK 1 HAVE BOTH STARTED UP T-SHIRT SIDELINES THAT REFLECT THE COMPANIES' HOUSE STYLE OF DESIGN, WHILE AVOIDING BEING TOO OBVIOUS A PIECE OF SELF-PROMOTION. LEFT PAGE: ALL DESIGNS BY PAUL HUMPHREY AND LUKE DAVIES AT INSECT, 1997–2000. THIS PAGE: ALL DESIGNS BY THINK 1, 2000.

UK LABEL GIMME 5 AND JAPANESE COMPANY GOODENOUGH BOTH STARTED UP IN THE EARLY 1990S. GIMME 5 FOUNDER MICHAEL KOPELMAN WAS A HUGE FAN OF STÜSSY GRAPHICS, AND SIMILARLY HIS LABEL USES FOUND IMAGERY AND REFERENCES TO POPULAR CULTURE. 01. DESIGNED BY GIMME 5, 1998. 02. DESIGNED BY GOODENOUGH, 1999.

PRODUCT 250 PICK A THEME FOR THEIR CLOTHING COLLECTIONS, WHICH ARE NONETHELESS ALL IMBUED WITH THE PUNK ETHOS OF "DO-IT-YOURSELF", HENCE THE HANDWRITING AND DELIBERATE CROOKED PRINT EFFECTS. 03&04. DESIGNED BY PRODUCT 250, 2000.

"THESE T-SHIRTS WERE INFLUENCED BY THE IMAGERY OF LATE-1960S AND EARLY-1970S RADICALISM IN FRANCE AND GERMANY AND ARE AN IRONIC / AMBIGUOUS TAKE ON THE CONCEPT OF CONSUMERISM AND THE POSITION OF 68–76 IN THE FASHION MARKET. IT'S TRYING TO GET PEOPLE WHO ARE IN FASHION TO THINK A BIT MORE (WITH IRONY!) NOT ALWAYS POSSIBLE," EXPLAINS FASHION LABEL 68–76 DIRECTOR, KENNETH MACKENZIE. 01&02. 1997.

FOR YEARS, MUSIC-RELATED MERCHANDISE WAS INEXTRICABLY LINKED WITH THE DESIGN OF AN ALBUM COVER GRAPHIC, WHICH WAS TRADITIONALLY STUCK ON THE FRONT OF A T-SHIRT WITH TOUR VENUE DETAILS LISTED ON THE BACK. SUCH T-SHIRTS ARE STILL COMMONPLACE TODAY, BUT AS CONSUMERS HAVE BECOME INCREASINGLY WISE TO THE MACHINATIONS OF RECORD COMPANY MARKETING DEPARTMENTS, THEY HAVE BECOME LESS CONTENT TO FALL FOR SUCH THINLY DISGUISED ATTEMPTS TO PART THEM FROM THEIR HARD-EARNED CASH. HENCE THE RISE AND RISE OF DESIGNERS SUCH AS STANLEY, WHOSE WORK WITH THE BAND RADIOHEAD CONTINUALLY INNOVATES AND ADDS SOMETHING FRESH AND UNSEEN TO ANY FAN'S WARDROBE. 03. DESIGNED BY STANLEY, W.A.S.T.E PRODUCTS LTD / RADIOHEAD, 2000.

I FIND PLAIN EXCITING

Portrait of a woman singing "Are Friends Electric?" by G. Numan in her head.

Love it.

ANTONI & ALISON HAVE ALMOST CORNERED THE MARKET IN CREATING FANTASTICALLY HUMOROUS, WITTY AND WARM-HEARTED T-SHIRTS WHICH TRAVEL SUCCESSFULLY ACROSS ALL CULTURAL AND LINGUISTIC BARRIERS. ANTONI BURAKOWSKI AND ALISON ROBERTS STARTED WORKING TOGETHER IN 1987, AND SINCE THEN THE T-SHIRT HAS BEEN ONE OF THEIR FAVOURITE MEDIA, WHILE THEY OFTEN MANAGE TO PRE-EMPT THE MOOD OF THE TIMES WITHIN EACH COLLECTION. EACH T-SHIRT HAS AN ELABORATE AND DETAILED STORY BEHIND IT, TO THE EXTENT THAT NOW THEY CREATE FILMS WHICH THEY PUT ON AT THEIR SHOWS: THE T-SHIRTS ACT ALMOST AS A SOUVENIR OF THE FILM, RATHER THAN BEING THE EXPECTED FOCAL POINT OF A CLOTHING COMPANY. SHOWN HERE ARE JUST A FEW OF THE HUNDREDS OF T-SHIRTS THE PAIR HAVE DESIGNED FROM THESE PARTICULAR COLLECTIONS: 01. SEASONAL GREETINGS, 1998. 02. ACTION, 1995. 03. WARM, 1991. 04. PORTRAITS, 1996. 05. ALL THE RAGE, 1992. 06. LOVE IT, 1993. 07. I FEEL AMAZING, FANTASTIC, INCREDIBLE, BRILLIANT, FABULOUS, GREAT, 1989.

LONDON-BASED COMPANY EINEKOIN HAS TAKEN THE IDEA OF CUSTOMIZATION TO AN EXTREME. PUNCHING HOLES IN MATERIAL, SPRAY-PAINTING GRAFFITI ONTO SHIRTS AND STICKING THEM UP WITH BLACK TAPE IS ALL PART OF THE SERVICE. 01. DESIGNED BY EINEKOIN, 2000. 02. AMUSING GRAPHICS FROM LONDON DESIGN FIRM, BUMP, 1999. 03. A PUN FROM MICKEY BRAZIL PLAYING ON THE IDEAS OF "TOOTING" COCAINE AND TOOTING, SOUTH LONDON. DESIGNED BY JULIE CUDDIHY AND DARREN HESLOP, MICKEY BRAZIL, 1996. 04. DESIGN COMPANY HYBRID REPLACED CHE GUEVARA TO PORTRAY KEN LIVINGSTONE AS LONDON'S WOULD-BE REVOLUTIONARY IN THE RUN-UP TO THE MAYORAL ELECTIONS IN 2000. 05. FAKE INCORPORATE RECYCLED CASHMERE INTO THEIR CLOTHING, A NEAT WAY OF MAKING THE T-SHIRT EVEN MORE DESIRABLE (THE ROSETTES ARE DETACHABLE). DESIGNS BY DESIREE MEYER, 2000.

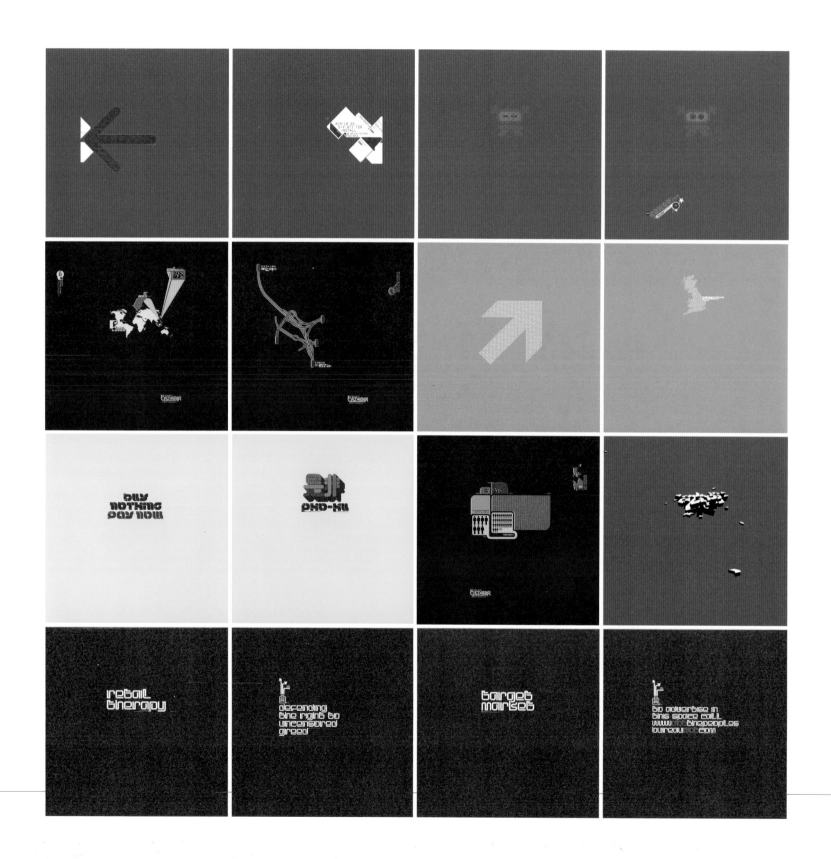

SHEFFIELD-BASED GRAPHIC DESIGN COMPANY THE DESIGNERS REPUBLIC HAVE MANUFACTURED THEIR OWN T-SHIRTS SINCE THE LATE 1980S, AS WELL AS DESIGNING HUNDREDS FOR BANDS SUCH AS POP WILL EAT ITSELF. THEY SELL THE SHIRTS THROUGH THEIR WEBSITE, <THEPEOPLESBUREAU.COM>, WHILE THEY ARE NOTEWORTHY FOR THEIR WRY, NORTHERN ENGLISH SENSE OF HUMOUR (SEE FOR EXAMPLE THE T-SHIRT CALLED "NORTH OF NOWHERE", WHICH HIGHLIGHTS SHEFFIELD ON A MAP OF BRITAIN). ALL DESIGNS BY THE DESIGNERS REPUBLIC, 2000.

FASHION LABEL THE DUFFER OF ST GEORGE STARTED LIFE AS A STALL IN CAMDEN MARKET, LONDON, BOTH SELLING AND REPRODUCING VINTAGE CLOTHING. THEIR DEBT TO EARLIER ERAS IS OBVIOUS, WITH THE APPROPRIATION AND RECYCLING OF TYPEFACES AND LOGOS A PARTICULAR THEME OF THEIR 2000 COLLECTION. ALL DESIGNS BY MARCO CAIRNS, 2000.

01 02 03 SYDNEY-BASED ILLUSTRATOR AND GRAPHIC DESIGNER PAUL MCNEIL HAS CREATED HUNDREDS OF T-SHIRTS IN HIS TIME, FOR THE LIKES OF MAMBO, HARD YAKKA AND
04 05 06 KIDDER. ALL DESIGNS BY PAUL MCNEIL. 01. TOUR T-SHIRT FOR US BAND, GUIDED BY VOICES, 2000. 02. CRACK KILLS, FOR MAMBO, 1996. 03. TIKI, FOR MAMBO, 1997. 04.
ABCD, FOR MAMBO, 1997. 05. HARD YAKKA 1, FOR HARD YAKKA, 1999. 06. KIDDER 2, 2000.

01 02 MORE WITTY DESIGNS FROM HOWIES: THE SHOPLIFTER SHIRT INCORPORATED AN ELECTRONIC BARCODE IN THE SLEEVE THAT SET OFF SHOP ALARM SYSTEMS, A COMMENT ON HOW OFTEN SCRUFFY-LOOKING YOUTHS ARE STOPPED BY SECURITY GUARDS. "THE SHIRT WAS BANNED FROM THE HIGH STREETS OF BRITAIN AND THE POLICE THREATENED TO CHARGE HOWIES WITH CAUSING A PUBLIC NUISANCE UNLESS WE STOPPED PRODUCTION. EEK," SAYS COMPANY CO-FOUNDER DAVID HIEATT. THEIR "BSE" T-SHIRT (BSE STANDING FOR BOVINE SPONGIFORM ENCEPHALOPATHY OR "MAD COW DISEASE") WAS THOUGHT UP DURING THE BRITISH BEEF CRISIS, THOUGH THE FAST FOOD COMPANY'S LITIGIOUS NATURE PREVENTED IT FROM BEING MASS MARKETED. CREATIVE DIRECTOR ON ALL DESIGNS WAS DAVID HIEATT. 01. SHOPLIFTER, DESIGNED BY DAISY CRESSWELL. 02. BSE, DESIGNED BY NEIL CRADDOCK, 1995–2000.

BASIC COMMUNICATIONS — by bump

"Make-Your-Own Message" KIT

Create & wear your own message by blacking out digital cells.

[Includes : Permanent Marker Pen]

デジタルセルを塗りつぶして自分自身のメッセージを着よう!!

[パーマネント・マーカー付]

Message Samples — 文字例

trY- hard *Try Hard*

900d IdER *Good Idea*

900d UI bE *Good Vibe*

FAt- SLA9 *Fat Slag*

run- rI OE *Run-Ride*

nOt- nI CE *Not-Nice*

HAUE FUn *Have Fun*

HOOO HAAA *Hooo Haaa*

2000 2001 *2000 2001*

ALPHABETS & NUMBERS

A a B b   C c D d   E e F f
G g H h   I i J j   H H L L
N n O o   P P 9 9   r r S S
t t U u   U u H H   y y z z
0 1 2 3   4 5 6 7   8 9 -

PRACTICE BELOW — 下書きシート

8888 8888 8888
8888 8888 8888
8888 8888 8888
8888 8888 8888

Instructions - 記入方法

1. First refer to "Message Samples" and "Alphabets Instruction" - see backside.
   まず文字例と裏面のアルファベット記入例をご覧ください。

2. Once you have your own message, first try it on the practice sheet.
   自分のメッセージが決まったら、まず裏面の下書きシートにトライ。

3. Now, you make your own message on your T-shirt while carefully looking at the sketch you made on the practice sheet.
   あとは、下書きを見ながらTシャツのセルを黒く塗りつぶすだけでOK。

※ Be careful when you black out the edge of the cells.
   セルの周囲を塗るときは注意深くていねいに。

※ Letters you cannot produce are "M" and "W".
   "M" と "W" の文字は作ることができません。

bump

"bump" is the London based graphic design unit of Mike Watson,(b. 1965), and Jon Morgan,(b. 1971). The first thing that strikes you about bump's work is its wicked humour and plundering of tabloid culture. But closer inspection reveals a surprisingly light touch and a well-considered sense of irony. Ideas are based on things that already exist - icons which are instantly recognizable such as till receipts, shopping trolleys, pints, fags, going down the dogs the choreography of domestic tows. It's the combination of the raw, the wicked, and the banal which inspires observations of everyday things and the behaviour that surrounds us, usually missed by most of us who don't seem to notice the detail. Bump point out the details, isolating and repositioning it with a sharp sense of irony which simultaneously celebrates and disturbs.

パンプ

ロイヤル・カレッジ・オブ・アート〔王立美術校〕の同級生、マイク・ワトソンとジョン・モーガンのデザイン・ユニット、"バンプ"。彼らの得意技は「アブない・ユーモア」と「イギリス特有のタブロイド紙・カルチャーのエッセンス」。時として初めて見る者に対して強烈なインパクトを伴っているが、よく見ると、けっしてヘビーなものではなく、「どこか気づかいのある皮肉」あるいは「人畜無害のブラック・ユーモア」であり、それが"かるい・ジョブ"のように彼らの制作するイメージに魅力を与えている。日常の都市生活の中で目にするモノや行為を素材にして"鋭い皮肉センス"で料理している。Harvey NicholsやKnollなどとのプロジェクトをこなす一方、最大手広告代理店 Saatchi & Saatchiの社長へ痛烈な皮肉を込めたメッセージを送りつけるなど、ブラック・ユーモア・テロリストとしても活躍（?）している。「アブない・ユーモア」で単に遊んでいるだけに見えるかもしれないが、マイク曰く「僕たちが作るすべてのイメージと僕たちの行為すべてが意味を持っている。」この二人の作品、実はとても真剣に「アブない・ユーモア」をクリエイトしている。

© bump, london : Gingham Inc

Produced and distributed by Gingham Inc. Japan : t. 81-92-734-5420 f. 81-92-734-5779 e. info@gingham.com

04 05 06   01 02 03   01&02. GRAPHIC DESIGNERS BUMP TAKE THE IDEA OF CUSTOMIZING YOUR OWN T-SHIRT TO AN EXTREME WITH THIS RATHER CLEVER "MAKE-YOUR-OWN MESSAGE" KIT. SUPPLIED WITH A PEN AND A T-SHIRT PRINTED WITH A SERIES OF EIGHT DIGITAL CELLS, THE PROUD OWNER CAN BLOCK VARIOUS PARTS OF EACH ONE OUT IN ORDER TO CREATE THEIR OWN SLOGAN. SUGGESTIONS INCLUDE "FAT SLAG" AND "HAVE FUN". DESIGNED BY BUMP, 1999. PRODUCED BY GINGHAM INC., JAPAN.

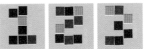

03. SKIM.COM IS A VERY 21ST-CENTURY COMPANY: CLOTHING AND ACCESSORIES ARE ALL STAMPED WITH A UNIQUE WEB ADDRESS, SO ANYONE WHO SPOTS YOU CAN THEN WRITE YOU A MESSAGE. THE ADDRESS SHOWN HERE IS 100% COTTON'S VERY OWN MAIL BOX, SO FEEL FREE TO DROP US A LINE. 04–06. CLEAR, SIMPLE DESIGNS: ORIGAMI PAPER WAS USED TO PRINT THESE T-SHIRTS FOR JAPANESE CLOTHING LABEL, SATANARBEIT. DESIGNED BY SUBTLE RUKUS, 2000.

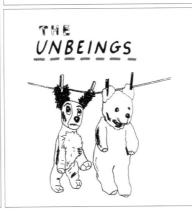

ERIC HAZE STARTED OUT AS A GRAFFITI ARTIST IN NEW YORK IN THE 1970S AND HAS WATCHED AS GRAFFITI MOVED FROM BEING A SUBVERSIVE FORM OF STREET EXPRESSION TO AN ACCEPTED PART OF THE ART ESTABLISHMENT. HAZE'S SIGNATURE REMAINS A FOCAL PART OF HIS DESIGN: "TO ME, ONE OF THE BEAUTIES OF GRAPHIC AND PRODUCT DESIGN IS THAT YOU CAN USE DIFFERENT STYLES OR CONCEPTS FOR EACH PIECE, AS LONG AS IT WORKS FOR THAT IDEA: IT DOES NOT NECESSARILY HAVE TO HAVE A DIRECT RELATIONSHIP TO PAST WORK," HE EXPLAINS. 01. DRIP TAG, 1998. 02. CUSTOM BUILT, 1993. 03. BAT-HAZE WAS THE FIRST T-SHIRT HAZE PRODUCED, IN 1986. IT WAS ORIGINALLY SOLD IN KEITH HARING'S POP SHOP IN NEW YORK. 04. EXPLOSION, 1994. 05. HAZE STROBE, 1996. 06. HAZE-AM, 2000. 07. CAMO-TAG, 1997. 08. INDUSTRIAL, 1992. 09. JUICY, 1995. 10. HAZE LEAGUE, 1997. 11. H-STRIPE, 1993. 12. WILD HAZE, 1995. 13. EL HAZE, 1997. 14. LONDON-BASED ILLUSTRATOR PAUL DAVIS USES THE T-SHIRT AS A MEANS OF COMMUNICATING HIS WRY OUTLOOK ON LIFE TO A WIDER AUDIENCE, 1999–2000.

100% COTTON

THE BRIEF WAS SIMPLE: DESIGN A GRAPHIC ON THE THEME OF 100% COTTON, WHICH WE COULD THEN PRINT ONTO A PLAIN WHITE T-SHIRT. THE WILDLY DIFFERENT RESULTS NOT ONLY SHOW THE HUGE VERSATILITY OF THE T-SHIRT, BUT ALSO PROVIDE A SHOWCASE OF EXCLUSIVE AND ORIGINAL WORK FROM SOME OF THE BEST GRAPHIC TALENTS AROUND. ENJOY.

BEN NOTT, DESIGNER, USA

"THE IDEA IS THAT THIS IS A FRAMED PIECE OF ART (ALL WHITE T-SHIRT MATERIAL). THE PIECE IS CAPTIONED 'A PICTURE OF 100% COTTON.'"

DAVE KINSEY, GRAPHIC DESIGNER, USA

"I WOULD SAY THE REASON FOR THE PAINT STROKES AND ILLUSTRATED T-SHIRT IS TO REFERENCE ART ON T-SHIRTS RATHER THAN BIG CORPORATE LOGOS. IN MY OPINION, THE BEST T-SHIRTS ARE CONCEPT SLOGANS THAT SPEAK ONE'S PERSONALITY, OR NICE FLUENT GRAPHIC ARTS AND ILLUSTRATIONS WITH PROPER COLOUR BALANCE THAT MAKE THEM A ONE-OF-A-KIND ITEM. A T-SHIRT IS A CANVAS AND A BILLBOARD, SO IT SHOULD SPEAK FOR ITSELF."

DENIS DULUDE, TYPOGRAPHER AND GRAPHIC DESIGNER, CANADA

"FIRST OF ALL, I'M A T-SHIRT FREAK. I REALLY ENJOY NICE GRAPHICS ON T-SHIRTS. I CHOOSE TO DESIGN IN ONE OR TWO COLOURS, WHILE I PREFER TO WORK WITH SPOT COLOURS. I REALLY ENJOY WORKING WITH TYPE, ESPECIALLY WHEN THERE ARE ONLY A FEW WORDS. I HAD THE COOLEST TIME DOING THIS PROJECT!"

INTRO, GRAPHIC DESIGN AGENCY, UK

"A VISUAL DOUBLE-TAKE, IN THAT IN ONE SIMPLE MOVE THE '100' CAN BE SHIMMIED TO BE A PERCENTAGE SIGN. GRAPHIC TRICKERY USING THE REPETITION OF SHAPES."

MARKUS WEISBECK, GRAPHIC DESIGNER, GERMANY

"PRINTED SHIRTS ARE SO POPULAR, YOU FIND ALL KINDS OF THEMES PRINTED ONTO THEM. THE IDEA HERE WAS TO USE AN INTERNET SEARCH SITE (SUCH AS YAHOO!), WITH ITS SPECIAL CLASSIFICATION SYSTEM TO SHOW OFF THE DIFFERENT USES OF T-SHIRTS. AT THE END OF EACH PATH YOU'LL FIND THE SAME PRINTED SHIRT."

PAUL FRANK INDUSTRIES, FASHION LABEL, USA

"JULIUS, THE MONKEY, IS ONE OF OUR CHARACTERS. HE'S A MISCHIEVOUS AND CHEEKY MONKEY. ILLUSTRATION WAS BY PARKER JACOBS."

PAUL MCNEIL, GRAPHIC DESIGNER AND ILLUSTRATOR, AUSTRALIA

"COTTON IS ONE OF THE DULLEST THINGS IN THE WORLD. THIS WAS THE ONLY FUNNY WAY I COULD THINK OF INCORPORATING IT. AND I DID IT TO MEET GIRLS. I JUST DO THINGS TO MAKE PEOPLE HAPPY, REALLY."

SHEPARD FAIREY, GRAPHIC DESIGNER, USA

"I'M JUST LOOKING FOR ANY EXCUSE TO PERPETUATE MY ABSURDIST PROPAGANDA AND T-SHIRTS ARE THE PERFECT CANVASES. I LIKE TO EMPLOY THE SOUND DESIGN PRINCIPLES AND BOLD COLOURS OF RUSSIAN CONTRUCTIVISM. I LOOSELY ADDRESS THE '100% COTTON' MEDIUM-IS-THE-MESSAGE ISSUE BY INCORPORATING A STITCHED THREAD MOTIF IN THE DESIGN."

HOWIES, CLOTHING COMPANY, UK

"MAKING COTTON IS AN UGLY PROCESS. THE IRONY IS WE ALL THINK COTTON IS ONE OF THE MOST NATURAL THINGS AROUND. SO WE JUST THOUGHT IT WOULD BE AN IDEA TO WRITE THAT PROCESS DOWN ON A T-SHIRT, WARTS AND ALL. IT DIDN'T MAKE PRETTY READING OR A GREAT T-SHIRT IF TRUTH BE TOLD, BUT IT DID MAKE US VOW TO ONLY USE ORGANIC COTTON IN THE FUTURE."

THINK 1, GRAPHIC DESIGN AGENCY, UK

"IT WAS FOR THE INSIDE LABEL, LOOKING AT MATERIAL INSTRUCTIONS / PERCENTAGES. IT WAS A PISS–TAKE OF THE WHOLE 'STATEMENT ON T-SHIRT THING', WHERE THERE IS OFTEN AN ELEMENT OF IRONY, OR AT LEAST ON OURS THERE IS. THE OPPORTUNITY TO SHOUT IT OUT LOUD ADDS A SPURIOUS WEIGHT TO WHAT YOU'RE SAYING. IS IT REALLY SO IMPORTANT THAT YOU NEED TO PUT IT ON A T-SHIRT? IT'S SILENT SHOUTING / T-SHIRTS AS A COMPETITION IN WIT."

ALEXANDER GELMAN, GRAPHIC DESIGNER, NEW YORK

"I HAVE ALWAYS BEEN OBSESSED WITH CHARTS AND DIAGRAMS, ATTRACTED TO THE VISUAL REPRESENTATION OF ANY COMPLICATED INFORMATION. THE LANGUAGE OF CHARTS HAS AMAZING AESTHETIC QUALITIES BASED ON ITS FUNCTIONAL NATURE. ASKED TO INTERPRET '100% COTTON', IT WAS NATURAL TO ENGAGE THIS CHART LANGUAGE."

'100% cotton wool ball'. Antoni & Alison. 2000.

ANTONI & ALISON, FASHION DESIGN LABEL, UK

"WE REFERENCE COTTON WOOL BALLS IN OUR OWN WORK AND WE WANTED TO MAKE THIS PIECE SOFT, SO WE PUT ONE ON A RABBIT AS A TAIL. THE MILLENNIUM FABRIC, WHICH WAS ALSO 100% COTTON, DATED THE PIECE PERFECTLY."

PETE FOWLER, ILLUSTRATOR, UK

"THE 'AUTOMATIC DRAWING DWARF' SCRIBBLES IN STEREO, ITS SPIRIT POSSESSED BY 'MONSTERISM' (THE STATE WHERE ONE IS 'MONSTERIZED')."

THOMAS BARWICK, ILLUSTRATOR, UK

"IT'S ON THE WRONG SIDE OF KRAZY TOWN, BUT IT DOES MAKE ME LAUGH. THE RAT IS ACTUALLY REALLY HAPPY, SO THAT'S WHY IT'S OKAY TO LAUGH AT HIS PLIGHT AS EVIL SCIENTISTS MAKE COTTON GROW OUT OF HIS TUMMY."

TIM FLETCHER, DESIGNER, UK

"TAKING COTTON REELS AND THE REPEATED PATTERNS THAT APPEAR IN COTTON WHEN IT'S WOVEN AS A STARTING POINT, I CREATED THIS SIMPLE TYPEFACE."

ERIK BRUNETTI, FUCT CLOTHING LABEL, USA

"WELL, I WANTED IT TO LOOK ENGLISH, AN OLD ENGLISH LABEL LOOK. SOMETHING THE QUEEN WOULD BE PROUD TO WEAR ON HER OWN BUM – OR ANY DICTATOR, FOR THAT MATTER..."

KAREN SAVAGE, FASHION DESIGNER, LONDON

"USING WORD ASSOCIATION, I CAME UP WITH THE WORD 'KNICKERS': A GIRLY SWEARWORD AND A CHEEKY SLANG WORD FOR WOMEN'S UNDERWEAR. THE WEARER CAN BE ACTIVE, IRREVERENT AND HUMOROUS BY EXPRESSING HERSELF, STATING 'KNICKERS.'"

YACHT ASSOCIATES, GRAPHIC DESIGN AGENCY, LONDON

"INSIDE OUT... THE T-SHIRT THAT IS INFINITELY DIFFERENT. UNSEW, RESEW, REMOVE, REARRANGE – IT'S UP TO YOU."

100%
PICTURES

'No Fun.' - Antoni + Alison.

BUT ALSO WITH OUR PACKAGING, TO TURN IT INTO THE MOST MODERN PRODUCT," EXPLAINS ANTONI BURAKOWSKI. "WHEN WE STARTED, WE LOVED THE FACT THAT THE T-SHIRT WAS, AND STILL IS, SUCH A POPULARIST PIECE OF CLOTHING." ALL DESIGNS BY ANTONI & ALISON. 01. BE HAPPY, 1988. 02. I LOVE WINKY, 1997. 03. DAY TRIPPER, 1999. 04. I CAN FLY, 1994. 05. NO FUN, 2000.

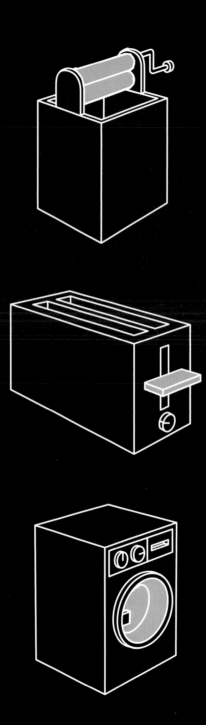

01–03. SIMPLE DRAWINGS OF EVERYDAY OBJECTS ADORN T-SHIRTS FROM LONDON DESIGN COMPANY FORM. ANOTHER SERIES THEY PRODUCED BORE THE ICONS "PIE" AND "MASH". ILLUSTRATIONS BY JOHN SIDDLE, ART DIRECTION AND DESIGN BY PAUL WEST, PAULA BENSON AND JOHN SIDDLE, 2000. MEANWHILE, THE WORK OF ILLUSTRATOR PETE FOWLER IS OFTEN POPULATED BY WEIRD AND WONDERFUL MONSTERS, WHO TURN UP IN HIS REGULAR WORK FOR BAND SUPER FURRY ANIMALS, AS WELL AS IN HIS DESIGNS FOR TOKYO MUSIC MAGAZINE SNOOZER. 04–06. PETE FOWLER FOR SNOOZER, 2000.

BROTHERS STEPHEN AND ROBERT BLISS STARTED THE LABEL STEROID IN 1997 AND CREATE TRADEMARK GOTHIC-STYLE GRAPHICS WITH A TWIST. 01. HULK WITH MULLET, 1997. 02. APE CITY ROLLERS, 1997. 03. JAZZ BIRD, 1998. "THE COLOURS ARE 70S JUNK FOOD AND THE BIRD IS A 1950S ILLUSTRATION-STYLE PIGEON. I HATE PIGEONS, SO I THOUGHT I'D USE THIS ICON AS THE LABEL SYMBOL TO ANNOY MYSELF," STEPHEN BLISS EXPLAINS. 04. STEROID DEVIL, 1999. 05. BIBA HEAD, 1999.

mambo

particular nasty weather

LIKE RABBITS

MAMBO
TUBE RIDE

simple footpath
humour #2

IRREVERENT SURFWEAR FIRM MAMBO HAS DONE MORE THAN MOST IN THE WAY OF DESIGNING T-SHIRTS, CREATING MORE THAN 70 NEW DESIGNS A YEAR FROM 1986
ONWARDS. HUMOUR IS PREVALENT THROUGHOUT THEIR DESIGNS, WHICH AFFECTIONATELY MOCK AUSTRALIAN STEREOTYPES AND OFTEN FEATURE RISQUÉ IMAGERY
THROWN IN FOR GOOD MEASURE. 01, 02, 04. DESIGNED BY PAUL WORSTEAD. 03. DESIGNED BY MATTHEW MARTIN. 05, 06. DESIGNED BY JIM MITCHELL. 07. DESIGNED
BY MARK FALLS. MAMBO, 2000.

01–02. KAREN SAVAGE DESIGNED SOME AGGRESSIVE T-SHIRTS AFTER A FEW BAD WAITRESSING EXPERIENCES. "I GOT THIS VERY ANGRY IDEA OF TAKING TWO MOUTHS AND STICKING THEM ON MY TITS," SHE EXPLAINS. "IT WAS TAKING THE CLASSIC ROLLING STONES IMAGERY THAT BIT FURTHER: IT WAS IN-YER-FACE, ANGRY, AGGRESSIVE AND SEXY AT THE SAME TIME. IT WAS ABOUT PUSHING YOURSELF RIGHT OUT THERE FIRST." SIMILARLY, ANOTHER OF HER DESIGNS, FINGERS, TOOK A COMMON OFFENSIVE GESTURE AND GAVE IT A TWIST: "THE NAILS ARE PAINTED AND WELL MANICURED, THE WOMAN IS WEARING A BIG DIAMOND RING AND A PEARL

BRACELET. IT WAS ANGRY, BUT DRESSED-UP AND GLAMOROUS AT THE SAME TIME." DESIGNS BY KAREN SAVAGE. 01. FINGERS, 1995. 02. MOUTHS, 1993. 03&04. TWO DESIGNS FROM FAKE. THE SMILEY FACE IS MADE OUT OF CASHMERE, WHILE THE ILLUSTRATION IMAGE COMES FROM A BRITISH NEWSPAPER MASTHEAD. DESIGNS BY DESIREE MEYER. 03. FINIS, 1998. 04. SMILEY FACE, 1997.

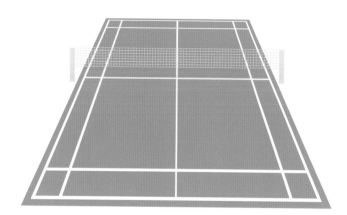

supersonic wave comes from extra.

LOVE TENNIS™

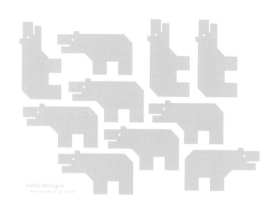

extra designs

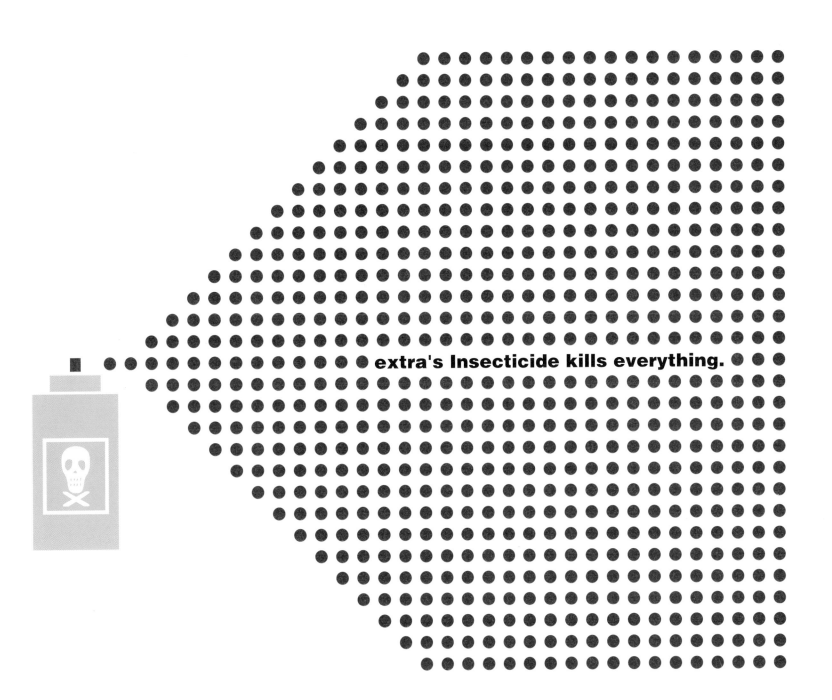

extra's Insecticide kills everything.

"WE MAKE THE GRAPHICS AS SIMPLE AS POSSIBLE. ALSO, WE TRY TO MAKE WHAT WE WANT TO PUT ON OURSELVES; IF WE ARE SATISFIED WITH THE GRAPHICS, THERE ARE AT LEAST SOME PEOPLE ON THE EARTH WHO MIGHT WANT TO BUY THE T-SHIRTS," EXPLAINS SHIN SASAKI OF JAPANESE DESIGN FIRM EXTRA. 01. EXTRA, 1998. 02. REPLY, 1999. 03. LOVE TENNIS, 1999. 04. LIME BEAR, 1998. 05. WAVE, 1999. 06. SPRAY, 1999.

OBEY

THE GOD OF THUNDER & ROCK N' ROLL

INSPIRED BY RUSSIAN CONSTRUCTIVIST IMAGERY, SAN DIEGO-BASED GRAPHIC ARTIST SHEPARD FAIREY HAS SPENT THE PAST FEW YEARS FLY-POSTING ENTIRE CITIES WITH STICKERS, POSTERS AND THE LIKE EMBLAZONED WITH THE IMAGE OF FORMER WRESTLER, ANDRE THE GIANT. HE'S ALSO MADE T-SHIRTS PRINTED WITH THE IMAGERY, DESIGNED TO MAKE PEOPLE QUESTION THEIR UNTHINKING LOYALTIES TO BRANDS AND ORGANIZATIONS. ALL DESIGNS BY GIANT / SHEPARD FAIREY. 01. BIG BROTHER, 1999. 02. OBEY FACE, 1997. 03. OBEY ISLAM, 1999. 04. RIOT COP, 1999. 05. OBEY ROCK, 1999.

01–12. ALL DESIGNS BY JAPANESE COMPANY HIROPON FACTORY. 01&09. 2000. 02–05&11. 1999. 10. 1994. 06. CO-DESIGNED WITH CHIHO AOSHIMA, 2000. 07. CO-DESIGNED WITH MR, 1998. 08. CO-DESIGNED WITH AYA TAKANO, 2000. 12. CO-DESIGNED WITH PAPER SHOP, 1998.

01. PRODUCT 250 DESIGNED THIS T-SHIRT FOR THE UK RECORD LABEL WALL OF SOUND. "THEY ARE MASSIVE QUEENS PARK RANGER FANS AND WANTED A DESIGN FEATURING LEGENDARY FOOTY PLAYER STAN BOWLES," EXPLAINS DESIGNER, JUSTIN TAYLOR. 02. ANOTHER PRODUCT 250 T-SHIRT, SERGE WAS A PART OF A COLLECTION INSPIRED BY ALL THINGS FRENCH, 1998. 03&04. PLANET OF THE APES IMAGERY AND A GRAFFITI-ED NEW YORK SUBWAY TRAIN ARE TYPICAL OF THE IMAGERY APPROPRIATED BY THE FASHION LABEL FUCT. 03. PAINTING BY NUMBERS, 1999. 04. CRAZY TRAIN, 1997.

LOS ANGELES-BASED GRAPHIC DESIGNER ALEXEI TYLEVICH DESIGNS T-SHIRTS FOR HIMSELF AND OTHER FASHION LABELS, SUCH AS MAX STUDIO (LEFT PAGE) WHICH SPECIALIZES IN WOMENSWEAR. THESE DESIGNS "WERE MEANT TO BE PERCEIVED AS FAUX FRAGMENTS OF THE EARLY 80S," TYLEVICH EXPLAINS. PERISHABLE GOODS (RIGHT PAGE) IS AN ONLINE PROJECT DEALING WITH THE ISSUES OF THE RELATIONSHIP BETWEEN FASHION AND ART. THE ARTWORK WAS BASED ON HISTORICAL ICONS THAT WERE ORIGINALLY DESIGNED FOR PUBLIC USAGE AND HAVE SINCE BECOME UBIQUITOUS AND ANONYMOUS, SUCH AS OTTO NEURATH'S CHARTS, 1970S OLYMPICS SIGNAGE, OR E-COMMERCE HIEROGLYPHICS. "THE FAMILIAR ICONS WERE SLIGHTLY ALTERED TO CONJURE UP A LESS COMFORTABLE READING," SAYS TYLEVICH. ALL DESIGNS BY ALEXEI TYLEVICH, 2000.

01&02. FASHION LABEL BURRO STARTED LIFE BY PRINTING A T-SHIRT PLEA TO FOOTBALL FANS TRAVELLING TO ITALY FOR THE WORLD CUP IN 1990. T-SHIRTS REMAIN AN IMPORTANT PART OF THEIR COLLECTION. DESIGNED BY SU DENNEY AND OLAF PARKER FOR BURRO. 01. NO ALLA VIOLENZA, 1989. 02. MEMORY, 2000. 03&04. ABSTRACT SHAPES AND SIMPLE GRAPHICS ARE TYPICAL OF JAPANESE FASHION LABEL, DENIME. BOTH DESIGNS FROM 2000.

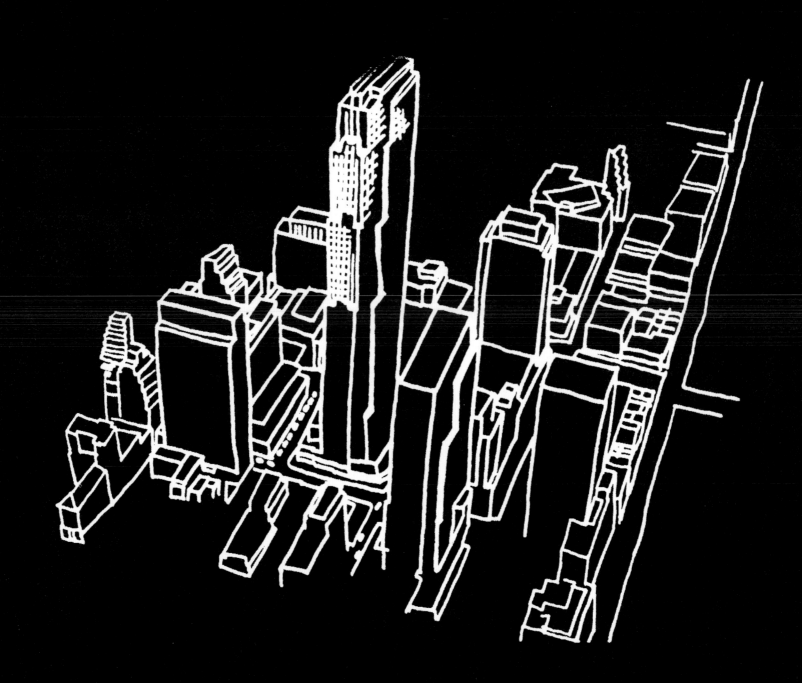

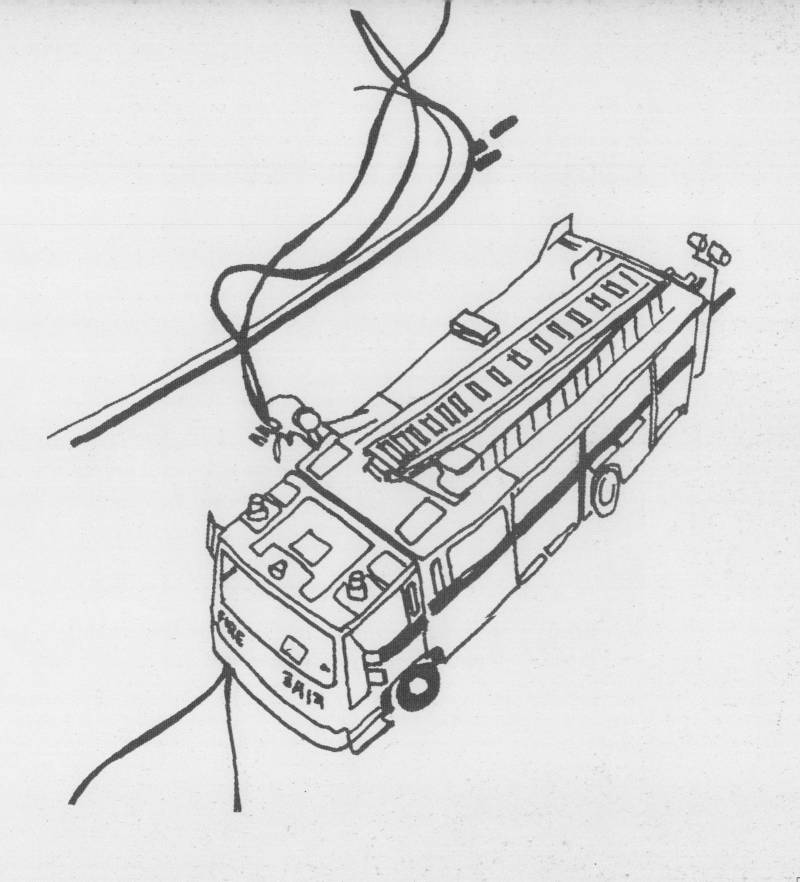

WONKY LINE DRAWINGS AND IMAGERY FROM EVERYDAY LIFE IN LONDON BECOME T-SHIRT ICONS FOR DESIGN COMPANY RUDE. BOTH DESIGNS BY ABI WILLIAMS AND RUPERT MEATS FROM RUDE, 2000.

01–04. IMMEDIATELY RECOGNIZABLE WARNING ICONS ARE GIVEN A TWIST BY LONDON-BASED FASHION DESIGNERS DAVE & JOE, 1997. 05–07. NEW YORK COMPANY TA MERE WAS FOUNDED ON MOTHER'S DAY, 2000 ("TA MERE" IS FRENCH FOR "YOUR MOTHER") BY TWO EX-PAT SWISS DESIGNERS, LAURENT FAUCHERE AND ANTOINE TINGUELY. THEIR HUGELY SIMPLE LOGO IS QUITE LITERALLY THEIR TRADEMARK: "THE CONTEMPORARY GRAPHICS, RELYING MAINLY ON TYPE, CREATE AN INTERESTING TENSION BETWEEN SLICK DESIGN AND STREET SLANG," COMMENTS TINGUELY. ALL DESIGNS, 2000.

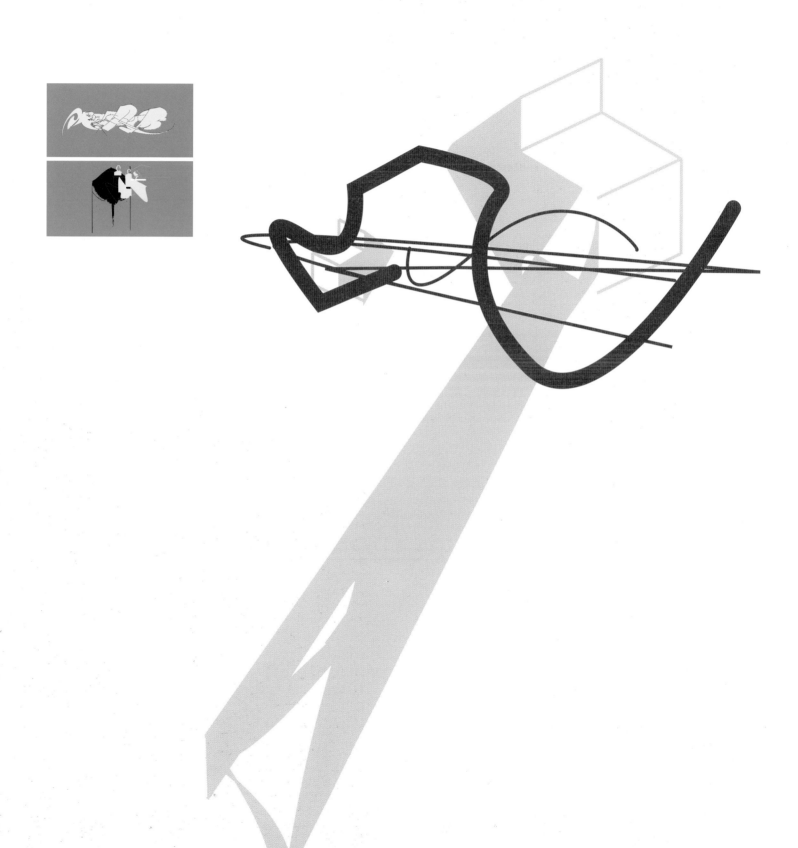

THESE ABSTRACT GRAPHICS WERE DERIVED FROM ORDNANCE SURVEY MAPS AND ARCHITECTURAL ILLUSTRATIONS, MAKING EYE-CATCHING AND ORIGINAL T-SHIRTS. DESIGNED BY KIRSTY THOMAS AT LIVERPOOL-BASED COMPANY, POST WITH THE NORTHERN SALOON AND SAM WIEHL, 2000.

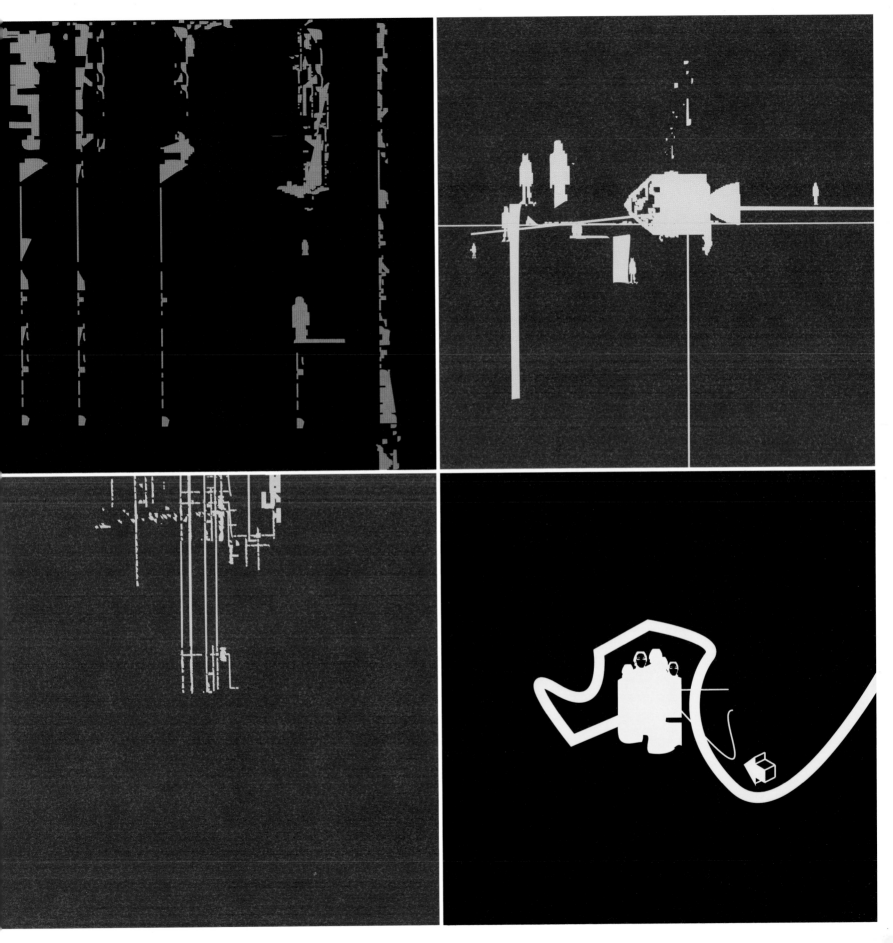

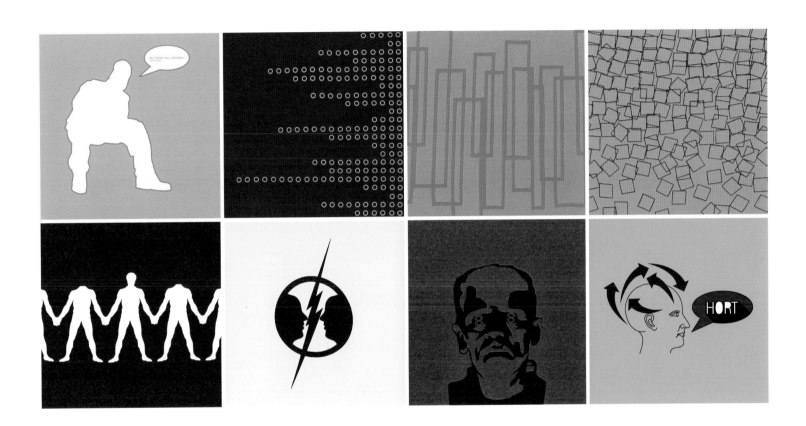

01. LONDON GRAPHIC DESIGN AGENCY INTRO MAKE T-SHIRTS FOR THEMSELVES, SUCH AS THE ONE SHOWN OPPOSITE. THEY SEND THEM OUT TO CLIENTS FOR CHRISTMAS PRESENTS, THOUGH THEY ALSO DESIGN MUSIC-RELATED MERCHANDISE FOR BANDS SUCH AS PRIMAL SCREAM. 02&09 DESIGNED BY GERMAN DESIGN COMPANY EIKESGRAPHISCHERHORT, 1999–2000. 03–05. ABSTRACT SHAPES FROM LONDON-BASED FASHION DESIGNERS ADAM AND CLAIRE PEARCE AT ALTERNATE CURRENT, 1998–99. 06–08. VEXED GENERATION. 06. CLONE CHAIN, 1998. 07. EYE TO EYE, 1998. 08. FRANKENSTEIN, 1997.

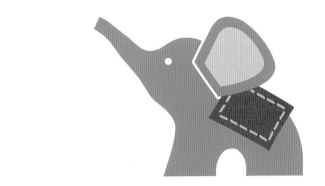

01&02. THOMAS BARWICK PUTS HIS SIMPLE BUT STRIKING ILLUSTRATIONS ONTO T-SHIRTS FOR A RANGE OF CLIENTS. 01. SPINACH WAS FOR A JAPANESE CLIENT, 2001. 02. MOD WAS DESIGNED FOR THE LAST CHANCE SALOON IN LONDON, 1999. 03–05. US-BASED COMPANY PAUL FRANK INDUSTRIES HAS A FAMILY OF CREATURES THAT ADORN EVERYTHING FROM T-SHIRTS TO TROUSERS, WALLETS TO PYJAMAS. THE MONKEY, JULIUS, IS THE MAIN PROTAGONIST, WHILE EACH ANIMAL HAS ITS OWN PERSONALITY, WHICH CAN BE EXPLAINED IN DETAIL BY FOUNDER AND CREATIVE DIRECTOR, PAUL FRANK. ALSO SHOWN HERE ARE CLANCY THE GIRAFFE AND ELLIE THE ELEPHANT.

01. ANDY JENKINS TOOK THE LOGO FOR HIS SKATEBOARD COMPANY, GIRL, AND TURNED IT INTO OLYMPIC EVENT ICONS. DESIGNED BY MICHAEL LEON, 1998. 02. DESIGNED BY CONRAD JOHNSON FOR LABEL, ROLLIN' STOCK, 2000. 03. FERGUS PURCELL GIVES MICHAEL JACKSON A PARTICULARLY FINE NEON GLOW IN THIS DESIGN FROM 2000. 04. "SLIP ON THE BLACK VINYL" – THIS RATHER SAUCY DESIGN WAS AGAIN BY FERGUS PURCELL FOR THE HEAVY METAL KIDS, 1998.

100%
COLLECTIONS

BEEN THERE, DONE THAT, BOUGHT THE T-SHIRT? TIM LEWIS, SENIOR DESIGNER AT UK STYLE MAGAZINE THE FACE CERTAINLY HAS. HE STARTED COLLECTING SOUVENIR T-SHIRTS FROM AROUND THE WORLD IN ABOUT 1990, AND THE RESULTS ARE CLASSIC KITSCH. A PARTICULAR FAVOURITE OF HIS IS THE "I'D RATHER BE IN THE HIMALAYAS" SHIRT: "GOLD FOIL BLOCK TYPE: COMPLETELY INAUTHENTIC, I'D IMAGINE," HE SAYS, BEFORE ADMITTING THAT MANY OF HIS SHIRTS HAVE COME FROM BRITISH CHARITY SHOPS AND HE'S NOT ACTUALLY AN INTERNATIONAL JETSETTER AFTER ALL.

Congratulations, you are now the owner of an "I am Spartacus" T-shirt. Wear it in the spirit of freedom, solidarity and rebellion for which it is intended. Better still, take a picture of yourself with it on, shouting, reading, bathing, jumping, smiling, in a photo-booth, praying, eating, listening, digging, snogging, knitting, sleeping, falling, walking, water-skiing, whatever-ing. Then send it to: PO box 25355, London, NW5 2FF. Your image will be added to the proud ranks and will be exhibited in 2001.

I AM SPARTACUS

AMSTERDAM-BASED ADVERTISING CREATIVE YANNAKIS JONES DESIGNED THIS T-SHIRT IN HOMAGE TO THE LATE STANLEY KUBRICK, DIRECTOR OF THE CLASSIC FILM SPARTACUS. THE SWING TICKET ON THE T-SHIRT CHALLENGES WEARERS TO SEND IN A PHOTOGRAPH OF THEMSELVES WEARING IT, AND JONES PLANS TO HOLD AN EXHIBITION OF THESE IMAGES. "THE ORIGINAL IDEA WAS TO FILL A WHOLE WALL WITH PICTURES. AN ARMY OF SPARTANS, IF YOU WILL. PEOPLE WHO UNDERSTAND THE REFERENCE RESPOND APPROPRIATELY: ONE FRIEND OF MINE ACTUALLY GAVE HIS T AWAY TO A STRANGER IN A CLUB AFTER SEVERAL HOURS OF HAVING THE SLOGAN YELLED BACK AT HIM," HE EXPLAINS. TYPOGRAPHY WAS BY JULIAN MOREY. 1999–2000.

T-SHIRT CLUBS ARE NOT EXACTLY NEW: PARTNERS MARK LEWMAN, ART DIRECTOR OF GIRL SKATEBOARDS, ANDY JENKINS AND SPIKE JONZE, FILM-MAKER, FOUNDED ONE CALLED CLUB HOMEBOY IN THE LATE 1980S THAT REACHED THE 10,000 MEMBER MARK BEFORE FOLDING IN 1990. "IT WAS EASY TO DO, CHEAP, AND A GOOD OUTLET FOR SILLY IDEAS," REMEMBERS JENKINS NOW. DESIGN COMPANY AIRSIDE HAS FORMULATED A SIMILAR PLAN, WITH A RANGE OF FOUR T-SHIRTS FROM RESPECTED MEMBERS OF THE DESIGN FRATERNITY AVAILABLE TO MEMBERS EACH YEAR. TOP GRAPHIC DESIGNERS LIKE TOM HINGSTON (MASSIVE ATTACK, ROBBIE WILLIAMS) AND IAN SWIFT (STRAIGHT NO CHASER, SWIFTY TYPOGRAFIX) HAVE ALL CONTRIBUTED: T-SHIRTS SHOWN ON THIS PAGE WERE DESIGNED BY IAN SWIFT, FRED DEAKIN, RIAN HUGHES AND PETE FOWLER.

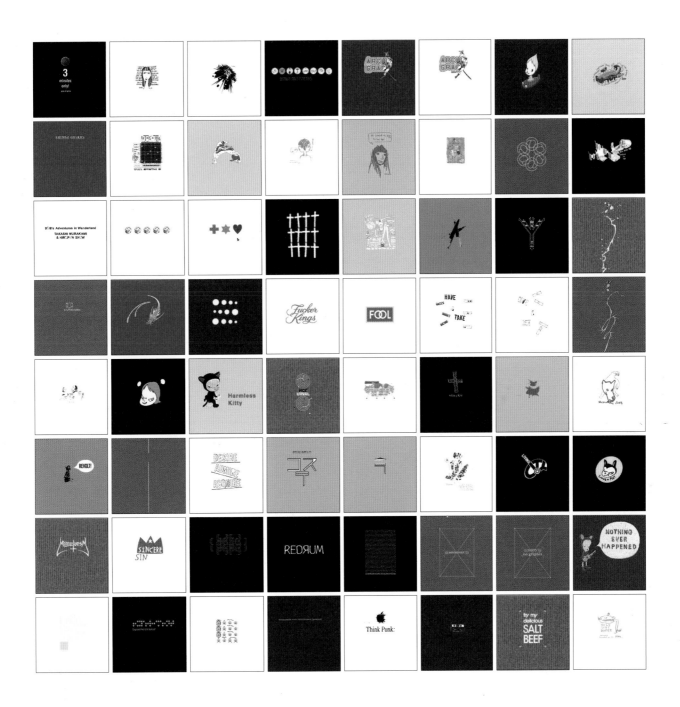

JAPANESE COMPANY 2K BY GINGHAM INC. SPECIALIZES IN SUPPLYING T-SHIRTS PROMOTING SHOWS AT INTERNATIONAL MUSEUMS AND ART GALLERIES AS WELL AS COMMISSIONING NEW WORK FROM CUTTING-EDGE DESIGNERS FROM AROUND THE WORLD. "THE ULTIMATE WAY OF HAVING SELF-IDENTIFICATION IS TATTOOING," SAYS DIRECTOR YOSHI KAWASAKI. "BUT MOST PEOPLE ARE NOT BRAVE ENOUGH FOR THAT. WEARING T-SHIRTS IS A MUCH EASIER WAY. IN OUR INCREASINGLY URBAN LIVES, THEY ARE ONE OF THE MOST EFFECTIVE TOOLS FOR EXPRESSING SELF-IDENTIFICATION AND HAVING A VISUAL COMMUNICATION." T-SHIRTS SHOWN ON THIS PAGE WERE DESIGNED BY: TYCOON GRAPHICS; KATSUNORI AOKI; ARCHIGRAM; YOSHITOMO NARA; GROOVISIONS; TAKASHI MURAKAMI; KASSIWA SATOH; LAWRENCE WEINER; SHINRO OHTAKE; TAKASHI KOMATSU; EXPERIMENTAL JETSET; MARGARET KILGALLEN; KAZUNARI HATTORI; ALEX RICH; KUSHY; ANDY WARHOL; H. C. ERICSON; BEA UUSMA SCHYFFERT; LOTTA KÜHLHORN; KLARA; LOMO; KAREN KILIMNIK AND JEFFREY FULVIMARI.

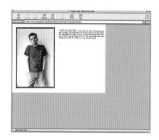

DUTCH PHOTOGRAPHER DANIELLE VAN ARK HAS BEEN PHOTOGRAPHING PEOPLE WEARING THEIR FAVOURITE ROCK MUSIC-RELATED T-SHIRT SINCE FEBRUARY, 2000. THESE IMAGES ARE THEN POSTED UP ONTO HER WEBSITE, <WWW.ILOVEMYSHIRT.COM>. "I STARTED THE PROJECT BECAUSE I READ A LOT OF MAGAZINES WHICH ALL FEATURED FAKE, HIP ROCK MODELS WITH NO CLUE, WHO WERE WEARING VINTAGE ROCK SHIRTS THAT YOU CAN BUY AT CERTAIN SHOPS FOR $50 OR MORE. IT BECAME A TREND AND PEOPLE STARTED WEARING, SAY, MOTORHEAD SHIRTS BECAUSE IT WAS THE COOL THING TO DO. I ALWAYS WANTED TO STEP UP TO THOSE PEOPLE AND ASK IF THEY COULD NAME THREE ALBUMS BY THE BAND. BUT OF COURSE I DIDN'T DO THAT, SO OUT OF FRUSTRATION I STARTED TAKING PICTURES OF REAL PEOPLE WITH A REAL LOVE FOR THE MUSIC." SHE PUTS THESE PICTURES UP ONTO THE SITE ALONG WITH THEIR REASONS FOR LIKING THAT PARTICULAR SHIRT SO MUCH.

CLOTHING LABEL PRODUCT 250 CHALLENGED 30 OF THEIR PEERS TO DESIGN A T-SHIRT FOR AN EXHIBITION THEY PUT ON IN LONDON IN 2000. SOLUTIONS RANGED FROM TRADITIONAL SCREENPRINTS TO GRAFFITI (ALSO SPRAYED ONTO THE GALLERY WALL), TO AN ENTIRELY DECONSTRUCTED T-SHIRT BY THE LABEL PROFESSOR HEAD, WHICH UNRAVELLED THE COTTON AND WOVE IT INTO THE SHAPE OF A BICYCLE. "WE'VE ALWAYS THOUGHT THAT THE T-SHIRT IS PRETTY MUCH LIKE POP ART," SAYS PRODUCT 250 CO-FOUNDER JUSTIN TAYLOR. "IT'S THE IDEA OF A WHITE CANVAS. IT'S CHEAP, DISPOSABLE, AND THROWAWAY. ANYONE CAN BUY ONE FOR £30, BUT IT'S ALSO A WORK OF ART."

BATES MOTEL

FASHION DESIGNER CONRAD JOHNSON HAS BEEN BUYING T-SHIRTS SINCE THE MID-1980S, AND HAS NOW AMASSED MORE THAN 500 TRULY CLASSIC T-SHIRTS. "IT'S A LIFESTYLE THING," HE EXPLAINS. "YOU CAN RELATE STRAIGHT AWAY TO THE GRAPHICS ON A T-SHIRT." BUT WHERE DOES HE KEEP THEM ALL? WHY, IN A WALK-IN WARDROBE, OF COURSE. "IT'S RIDICULOUS REALLY," HE ADMITS, UNREPENTANTLY.

CO-FOUNDER OF LONDON CLOTHING LABEL SILAS, RUSSELL WATERMAN WORKED AT THE STORE SLAM CITY SKATES, LONDON, FOR OVER TEN YEARS. DURING THAT TIME, HE ACCUMULATED A VARIETY OF T-SHIRTS DESIGNED BY SOME OF THE SKATE / SURF CLOTHING DESIGN GURUS, INCLUDING FUCT, X-LARGE, SUPREME AND STÜSSY. ONE OF HIS FAVOURITES IS THE DESIGN (OPPOSITE PAGE) FROM A SHORT-LIVED, ULTIMATELY DOOMED COLLABORATION BETWEEN THE FIRST TWO OF THOSE DESIGNERS, A SHOP IN LOS ANGELES CALLED X-FUCT. "I KEEP SOME OF THEM BECAUSE THEY REMIND ME OF CERTAIN INDIVIDUALS OR CERTAIN TIMES, WHILE OTHERS ARE JUST AMAZING GRAPHICALLY," WATERMAN EXPLAINS. "SOME OF THE T-SHIRTS ARE A PIECE OF CULTURAL HISTORY BECAUSE SOME OF THOSE COMPANIES DID SO MUCH MORE THAN MAKE CLOTHES: IT'S MUSIC, ART AND EVERYTHING."

FOUNDER OF BRITISH FASHION LABEL RED OR DEAD, WAYNE HEMINGWAY HAS BEEN PLUNDERING CHARITY SHOPS AND THRIFT STORES IN SEARCH OF T-SHIRTS FOR YEARS. SHOWN HERE ARE A FEW FAVOURITES FROM HIS COLLECTION OF HUNDREDS, INCLUDING THE FANTASTICALLY POLITICALLY INCORRECT "NUKE A GAY WHALE FOR JESUS", WHICH HEMINGWAY LOVES "BECAUSE IT HAS EVERY SINGLE UN-PC THING ON IT. T-SHIRTS ARE LIKE CALLING CARDS." HE CONTINUES, "EVERYBODY IN THEIR LIFE HAS OWNED A T-SHIRT WITH A SLOGAN ON IT. THEY CUT ACROSS SOCIAL AND FASHION BARRIERS."

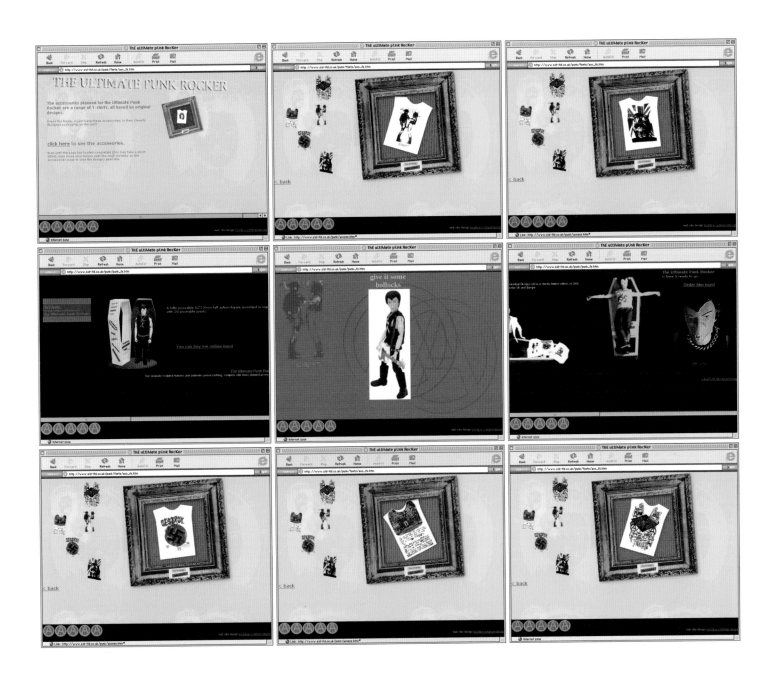

FROM THE MOMENT HE WAS STOPPED AND SEARCHED BY THE POLICE FOR BUYING A MALCOLM MCLAREN / VIVIENNE WESTWOOD–DESIGNED T-SHIRT BEARING THE IMAGE OF A RIPPED-UP UNION JACK WITH THE LEGEND "ANARCHY IN THE UK" EMBLAZONED ON IT, DESIGNER AND STYLIST DAVE CARROLL HAS BEEN A SELF-CONFESSED PUNK JUNKIE. AS A MARK OF RESPECT, CARROLL AND PARTNER NEIL HOLDHAM HAVE MANUFACTURED THESE PUNK ROCKER DOLLS, EACH ONE ACCOMPANIED BY A COMPLETE SET OF REPLICA MCLAREN / WESTWOOD-DESIGNED T-SHIRTS, IN PERFECT MINIATURE.

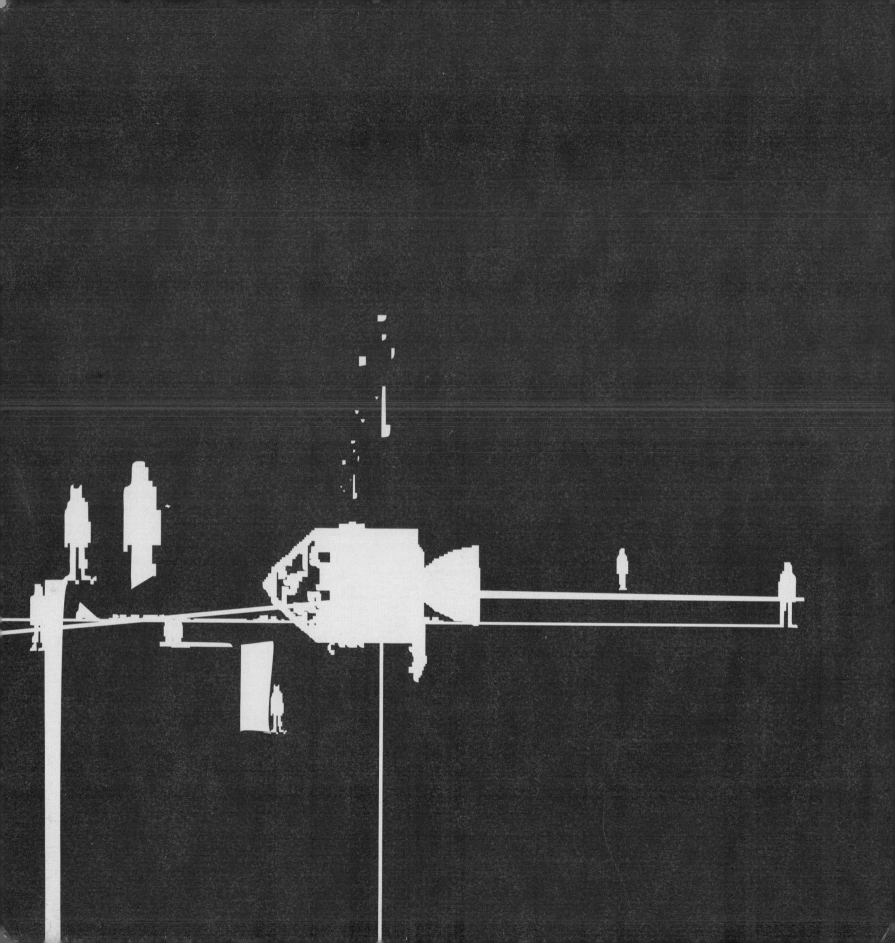